Dear Pitman Publishing Customer

IMPORTANT – Read This Now!

We are delighted to announce a special free service for all of our customers.

Simply complete this form and return it to the address overleaf to receive:

A Free Customer Newsletter

B Free Information Service

C Exclusive Customer Offers – which have included free software, videos and relevant products

D Opportunity to take part in product development sessions

E The chance for you to write about your own business experience and become one of our respected authors

Fill this in now and return it to us (no stamp needed in the UK) to join our customer information service.

Name: _____ Position: _____

Company/Organisation: _____

Address (including postcode): _____

_____

Country: _____

Telephone: _____ Fax: _____

Nature of business: _____

Title of book purchased: _____

Comments: _____

_____

-------------------------- | **Fold Here Then Staple** | --------------------------

We would be very grateful if you could answer these questions to help us with market research.

1 Where/How did you hear of this book?

☐ in a bookshop

☐ in a magazine/newspaper
(please state which):

_____

☐ information through the post

☐ recommendation from a colleague

☐ other (please state which):

_____

2 Which newspaper(s)/magazine(s) do you read regularly?:

_____

_____

_____

3 When buying a business book which factors influence you most?

(Please rank in order)

☐ recommendation from a colleague

☐ price

☐ content

☐ recommendation in a bookshop

☐ author

☐ publisher

☐ title

☐ other(s):

4 Is this book a

☐ personal purchase?

☐ company purchase?

5 Would you be prepared to spend a few minutes talking to our customer services staff to help with product development? YES/NO

The Business Publisher

Written for managers competing in today's tough business world, our books will help you get the edge on competitors by showing you how to:

- increase quality, efficiency and productivity throughout your organisation
- use both proven and innovative management techniques
- improve the management skills of you and your staff
- implement winning customer strategies

In short they provide concise, practical information that you can use every day to improve the success of your business.

FINANCIAL TIMES

PITMAN PUBLISHING

the Institute of Management

FOUNDATION

PITMAN PUBLISHING

Free Information Service
Pitman Professional Publishing
FREEPOST
128 Long Acre
LONDON
WC2E 9BR, UK

GETTING THE MOST FROM YOUR MARKETING SPEND

GETTING THE MOST FROM YOUR MARKETING SPEND

ALAN WOLFE

Director of Marketing Services
Primary Contact Limited

FINANCIAL TIMES

PITMAN PUBLISHING

PITMAN PUBLISHING
128 Long Acre, London WC2E 9AN

A Division of Longman Group Limited

First published in 1994

British Library Cataloguing in Publication Data
A CIP catalogue record for this book can be obtained from the British Library.

ISBN 0 273 60763 4

1 3 5 7 9 10 8 6 4 2

Typeset by Northern Phototypesetting Co. Ltd, Bolton
Printed and bound in Great Britain by
Biddles Ltd, Guildford and King's Lynn

*The Publishers' policy is to use paper manufactured
from sustainable forests.*

CONTENTS

PART C: SPECIAL TECHNIQUES AND SITUATIONS

FOREWORD

When I read the first draft of this book, I was so impressed that (much to the publisher's satisfaction) I ordered a large number of copies to send to all my staff and to many of my clients and friends.

It is a highly instructive book – yet eminently interesting and readable. This is because Alan Wolfe, through his broad experience and his scholarship, has developed a knack of avoiding impenetrable jargon: he identifies the key points of business strategy, marketing and advertising in a way readily understandable to someone who is not a specialist.

His chapter headings cover what I believe to be the most important subjects in marketing communications. And each of them can almost make the reader an 'instant expert' in its particular subject: briefing an agency successfully, understanding the nature and importance of a strong corporate image, finding a way of integrating the diverse parts of a marketing campaign or how to set about evaluating its results in cash terms.

Two chapters particularly impress me with their importance. The first is 'Why waste money on advertising?'. This is a vital subject, which I have never before seen addressed with such authority and conciseness.

The second is 'Setting a budget'. This discusses alternative techniques in common use, but with insight into the differing viewpoints of marketing and financial management, putting the case for both sides and a synthesis which should benefit both. It points out that 'any change in customer demand can affect prices and margins as well as sales volume. So advertising can be used to help in the recovery of "fixed overhead costs" at lower sales levels, as well as building higher sales volume when above the break-even point.' An interesting argument for a company struggling to maintain margins in the face of heavy competition or a market in recession!

Throughout his long and successful career at Ogilvy & Mather and its specialist 'business-to-business' agency Primary Contact, Alan has pioneered the evaluation of the effectiveness of campaigns. His approach to marketing communications (consumer or business-to-business) stems from a belief in the need to demonstrate cost-effectiveness, expressed in many chapters as 'advertising is a cost unless it sells'. His consistently analytical but pragmatic approach has produced many valuable insights into what works – and what does not.

I believe that all readers will benefit greatly from this book – and will enjoy reading it. I certainly did.

JOHN ARMITAGE
Chairman, Primary Contact Ltd
May 1994

INTRODUCTION

THE PRESSURE TO JUSTIFY

The advertising industry is everywhere under increasing pressure to justify its existence. This is not because business people are necessarily against it in principle. But advertisers' profits have been squeezed by increased competition, and their management are under strong pressures to keep costs down. Every form of expenditure, not just advertising, now has to be scrutinised to a greater extent than in the past.

In consequence, top management are asking their marketing specialists (both in internal departments and outside agencies) a series of difficult 'examination questions' which in effect require them to justify their advertising budgets. In the highly competitive Single European Market of the 1990s, spending more money on anything can be justified only to the extent that it helps sales and profits. Many of these questions can be summarised under the following five general headings:

Question 1: Advertising or product quality?

Advertising is the whole of any agency's life and income, no wonder they believe in it! But if it is only (say) 5 per cent of a typical advertiser's total costs, it can justify only 5 per cent of management's time, most of which has to be spent worrying about much bigger expenditures: raw materials, wages, production costs, transport, keeping the distributors happy. Will not getting these right (or wrong) have more effect on the survival and growth of the business than having even the most wonderful advertising? And will even the best advertising in the world sell a product if it is of poor quality or too expensive?

Question 2: What does success really mean?

Certainly *some* advertising works, or nobody would ever spend any money on it! But what does 'success' really mean? Even if an advertising campaign is shown to have a positive effect on sales, might it not be better to spend the money on cutting the price instead? Or would it be more profitable to hire more sales-people/use better ingredients/run a customer promotion/up-date the production machinery/automate the distribution network for Just-In-Time delivery?

Question 3: Can success be guaranteed in advance?

Every advertising agency has a portfolio of case histories of successes; many of the best of them have been published for all to read. But is everything those agencies do equally successful? Who shows the case histories of their failures? An advertiser who goes to a professional agency will find that all their work *looks* good, both the successes and the failures. Indeed, clients usually reject before they appear any campaigns that look incompetent, and therefore unprofessional agencies quickly go out of business. So, when presented with a new campaign, on what grounds other than appearance can the advertiser judge success from failure *before* approving it?

Question 4: Is advertising a current business expense or a long-term investment?

Finance departments classify money spent on items like machinery, raw materials and vehicles as an investment, because it produces something tangible which can be used over a period of time, which can be shown on the balance sheet as an asset and in bad times might even be sold for cash. Money spent on advertising has nothing tangible to show afterwards and so has to be classified as an 'expense' and written off in the current year's accounts. Expenses are the items a company keeps tightest control over, and the first things to be cut when short of cash or likely to fail to make the Return on Investment demanded by the suppliers of the company's fixed and working capital. Are the accountants right, and if not, how can they be convinced that advertising is an investment for the future?

Question 5: On what basis should a marketing budget be set, and how should it best be divided between alternative activities?

Once upon a time 'advertising to the customers' simply meant taking a few pages in newspapers and trade magazines. Now there is a much wider choice including television, posters, direct mail, print and video, telephone, trade fairs and exhibitions, and so on. Specialists talk about 'marketing communications' so as to include personal selling, public relations and sales promotion under the same heading. On what rational basis can a marketing budget be set and allocated between alternative techniques most profitably?

CAN THESE QUESTIONS BE ANSWERED?

These are all hard questions, and most people in the advertising industry in the past have ducked them, partly because of the genuine difficulty of separating the effects of advertising from the myriad other influences on sales, perhaps partly because of a fear that too much rigorous analysis might destroy advertising's greatest asset, its creativity.

At least one agency in the business-to-business sector has nevertheless grasped this nettle. Primary Contact are part of the worldwide Ogilvy Group, specialising in business and financial clients and supplying an ever-increasing range of marketing communications. As part of a public commitment 'consistently to produce measurably effective advertising', Primary Contact have built systems to measure the effects of advertising into all campaign plans. Learning by experience in this way has generated a number of general principles about what will (and will not) work, at least in the business-to-business and financial fields. Their application can consistently improve the chances of success of campaigns year by year.

These principles, interpreted through the collective knowledge and experience of the senior staff, have been written down as a series of short *Viewpoints*, originally for the mutual education of the agency and the continued improvement of its work. Since the first one, entitled 'Why waste money on advertising?', which set the tone for the series in 1986, *Viewpoints* now cover most aspects of planning, executing and evaluating a campaign.

They were later published for wider consumption, over 50 000 have been distributed, and demand for them continues. Rather than reprint them individually yet again, this book attempts to draw them all together in a logical sequence, edited only to minimise duplication, to expand on points made over-briefly and to add more examples where appropriate.

MARKETING AS A PROFIT-BASED ACTIVITY

This book is intended to illustrate the general principle that advertising (and other techniques of marketing communications) can be made accountable at least to the extent expected from other forms of business expenditure. The motto 'Advertising is a cost unless it sells' recurs throughout the book. It is a reminder that money spent by a business on advertising (or on anything else) which does not provide a fair return on investment (in the short or long run) is indeed money wasted; further, that missing opportunities for profit through spending too little or nothing at all also wastes money.

Avoiding such wastage is not easy, and requires a recognition that marketing is not just a set of techniques, but a philosophy of doing business which permeates all a company's activities. *Asset-based customer-orientated marketing* means using the assets of the company (people and money) to identify and satisfy customer needs in such a way as to generate a profit. All marketing activity can and must be planned and evaluated in as hard-headed and cost-conscious a way as any other business decision.

Getting the most out of marketing is based on three key factors:

(i)   understanding the buyer's decision-making process
(ii) integrating all aspects of the marketing campaign to achieve specific and realistic objectives
(iii) budgeting to maximise profit not minimise cost.

This book is designed to elucidate these factors.

THE NEED FOR BUSINESS PLANNING

Successful marketing does not happen in isolation – companies that are marketing-led can eventually find themselves in as much trouble as those which are product-led or finance-led. All three functions are interdependent on a Corporate Business Plan which specifies where the company is heading. In particular:

(i)   a 'mission statement' – namely, what the company believes its function to be and its place in the business community

(ii) the market target – who the desired customer is and the customer need to be satisfied

(iii) financial goals for the medium term – stated both qualitatively and in quantitative terms.

Clearly such objectives have to be set by top (general) management, although a wise company will seek input from its marketing specialists on the definition of the target market and to make sure that the required goals for revenue are realistic in the light of market conditions.

The safest basis for a business plan is a set of reliable and quantified forecasts of the market, the customers, the competition and the business climate in which all parts of the company will have to operate. These in turn are best derived from a Management Information System regularly up-dated with a range of internal data, published general economic and market facts and specific market research among current and potential customers.

Analysis of all these data in the light of the forecasts provides the three fundamentals for selecting a market-based business strategy: namely a Marketing Audit of the internal assets and resources at the disposal of the company, a Marketing Appraisal of the profit opportunities, risks and competitive problems faced in the external market, and an identification of the Key Factors for success. (I put a fuller discussion of these concepts and an approach to market-based business planning in *Profit from Strategic Marketing*, Financial Times/Pitman 1993.)

This book takes for granted that such a database and market forecasts exist and that a viable business plan has already been agreed. If they have not, then any form of marketing activity will be highly risky and liable to be cancelled or even put into reverse at any moment.

It is also assumed that the product supplied (the term here includes goods and services) is capable of satisfying the targeted customer need, is of a competitive quality and price, and (at least ideally) has some unique benefit to its customers in specification or price or image or in the range of pre- and post-sales services that surround most core products in business-to-business markets. If this is not true of the product, even the most creative of marketing campaigns will not generate repeat business or loyal customers. The supplier will then be drawn into an ultimately terminal spiral of price cutting, leading inevitably to re-building margins by reducing marketing activity, customer benefits and product specification, thereby making sales even harder to obtain (see Chapter 3).

THE SCOPE OF THIS BOOK

This book is designed primarily for the use of marketing management (and their bosses) particularly in companies selling to other businesses rather than to domestic households. Taken as a whole it is intended to stimulate strategic thought and discussion between marketing and general management: as an aid to improving the planning process, making the marketing function more cost-effective, leading to higher growth and profits for the whole operation.

Used tactically, individual chapters become training aids for internal marketing staff or part of the dialogue between them and their outside agencies and suppliers.

Part A deals with general strategic decisions such as developing a marketing strategy and corporate image or setting a budget and allocating funds between alternative activities in order to achieve revenue and profit targets. Part B deals with tactical aspects of executing a campaign and its subsequent evaluation. Part C covers some specific techniques or situations (such as database marketing or international advertising) which are not equally applicable to every company.

Each chapter (or *Viewpoint*) was originally written to stand alone, but they have here been run in a logical order so that readers who start with a later chapter on a topic of immediate interest should be aware that some of the basic premises which underlie the whole approach have been dealt with earlier in the book. This Introduction and the Conclusions summarise all that lies in between.

The word 'advertising' can usually be taken as a generic term for all forms of marketing communication between suppliers and customers of commercial products. The word 'product' is used throughout to signify both goods and services. Indeed, in business markets the distinction is becoming increasingly blurred, in that supplying a service usually requires the provision of a great deal of capital equipment, and supplying a good usually involves a number of pre- and post-sales services such as feasibility studies, installation, staff training, credit and helplines.

Author's note

I edited the whole of Primary Contact's *Viewpoint* series, and wrote most of them, but I must acknowledge with gratitude the help and input of many colleagues. In particular I thank Graham Bunting, Creative Director, for the original version of Chapter 8; Bill Swallow, Media Director, for Chapter 9; Tom Brannan, Client Service Director, for Chapters 15 and 16; and Tony Moore, Production Director, for acting throughout as guardian of the English language and good style. Above all I would like to acknowledge my great debt to John Armitage, Chairman, for initiating the *Viewpoint* concept, for his continued enthusiasm and encouragement in the production of the original series and for making possible this 'omnibus' version. However, I personally take ultimate responsibility for the content of this book and 'none of the above' should be held to blame for any heretical opinions expressed herein.

Part A

CAMPAIGN STRATEGY AND PLANNING

1

DEVELOPING A MARKETING STRATEGY

The best advertising stems from the best strategic thinking

THE PROBLEMS OF 'SHORT-TERMISM'

Advertising and other marketing activities often fail because of 'short-termism', namely, through using them only for tactical reasons, such as a cosmetic to hide some corporate weakness or to drum up sales in an unexpected down-turn. Such activity is soon cancelled, changed for a new idea, or its funds switched to something else; long before it has had time to make a proper impact on the customers, or indeed have any significant effect on the marketplace.

Yet companies are in business for the long term. They invest capital in assets which are written off over several years of active life, they provide contracts for their management and offer career prospects to their staff. This implies an expectation of regular sales income over these years. Advertising will be at its most effective if it is incorporated strategically into long-term plans so as to help generate a predictable level of sales.

Good strategic thinking is the vital foundation on which effective advertising is built. But such thinking will be good only if it is based on the four *fundamentals of marketing*. These are easier to state than to achieve:

(i)   You must provide the *right product* (good or service), at the right price and quality, for a market (or segment of one) of adequate size and potential.

(ii)   You must develop the *right distribution system* to make the product readily available to its target market, where and when they want it.

(iii) You must mount the *right advertising and promotional mix* to ensure that the target market is aware of, wants, and knows how to get your product.

(iv)   You must be dedicated to *looking after your customers*, not just during the buying process, but by satisfying their present and future needs. Sales for the long run mean building loyalty among *repeat* buyers. Each purchase sows the seeds of the next or poisons it. Customers not only 'vote with their feet'; they tell their family, friends, colleagues and business contacts that your product, or price or after-sales service is wonderful – or the reverse. Contented customers are the best sales force, and 'word-of-mouth' the most powerful advertising medium.

Good strategic thinking must cover each of these four fundamentals of marketing. If any link in the chain is weak or missing, the chain itself is weak, and will be highly vulnerable to the competition.

THE SOURCES OF STRATEGIC THINKING

The best strategic thinking stems from knowledge and a deep understanding of:

● *the advertiser's company*: its goods/services; strengths/weaknesses; business philosophy/goals/strategies; pricing policy; selling method/distribution chain; structure/problems/politics.

- *the market*: its structure and trends; the business climate; the competition; the opportunities and threats.
- *the customers*: which type and size of firms; how many of them; their locations; in what industries; their uses of your product; how it affects their output and its end-users.
- *the Decision Making Unit (DMU)*: who actually takes part in the purchase of your product, by job function, degree of influence and ideally by name. In business purchases the buying decision is rarely made by one person in isolation, even when there is a specialist 'purchasing department'. Different people with different job functions will specify, authorise and use the product, and even if few of them have ultimate power of choice more will have power of veto over a specific supplier who is unknown or has a bad reputation (see Chapter 2).
- *understanding why the advertiser needs to spend money on advertising*: the role of advertising in the marketing mix; how it integrates with other marketing activity; in what way advertising does its specific job better (or more cost-effectively) than any other marketing technique; how the effects of advertising contribute to the 'bottom line'.

RESEARCH

Research is often needed: to fill gaps in knowledge of the market; to identify the structure and membership of DMUs; to help understand customers' needs and perceptions; to help develop and evaluate marketing campaigns. Research is not a substitute for judgement – but can ensure that judgement is based on objective information rather than hunch. In developing the role of advertising within the marketing plan, advertisers should be aware of what research into markets, analysis of company data and codifying experience can show about what advertising is (and is not) capable of achieving.

For example, a research study (reported more fully in Chapter 4) shows that:

- products or services that are seen as being of relatively high quality earn higher prices and profits
- advertising affects perception of quality
- relative advertising pressure is related to market share
- businesses which invest in advertising obtain higher Return On Investment (ROI).

Analysis and experience (see Chapter 3) have shown that:

- a salesforce which is well supported sells more, and at better prices
- relatively small increases in sales volume often have a disproportionately large positive effect on bottom-line profits as fixed costs can be spread over a higher volume
- the bottom line is normally even more sensitive to firmer prices
- increasing demand normally encourages higher prices
- in almost all circumstances, price-cutting is an expensive alternative to effective advertising.

THE ROLE OF ADVERTISING

Advertising does not make sales on its own, save for exceptional circumstances such as a company which sells only by direct mail. It can nevertheless carry out a number of tasks which are essential preliminaries to making sales, and can support to make more effective other selling activities. It is essential to success to specify at the planning stage what the *prime role of advertising* is, and how this fits with the roles of other activities.

Appropriate roles include:

- raising awareness of a product among potential customers
- improving or changing the perceptions or image of a product or its supplier in the minds of the customers
- generating actual sales leads
- supporting the sales force or the distribution chain
- reassuring existing customers that they have made the right choice of supplier.

Advertising can play more than one such role at a time, but will be at its most effective if concentrated on one. Indeed, research shows that advertising which carries out its prime task successfully will create a 'halo effect' among the customers who will attribute to the product a number of other desirable characteristics.

ADVERTISING DOES NOT WORK IN ISOLATION

In business-to-business marketing it is rare to use a single technique to carry out all marketing communications tasks. Usually advertising needs to support and be supported by other techniques. All such marketing tools should be planned as an integrated part of a total campaign (see Chapter 7). For example:

(a) *Public relations* complements the role of advertising but cannot replace it. At its best it can be *more* powerful than advertising. But it is much less controllable in terms of timing, weight, repetition, continuity, and content of message. It can announce a new product or campaign most effectively. It generates more mileage from a media campaign, and used creatively can provide 'spin-off' activity. It can be targeted at otherwise hard-to-contact opinion formers such as technical gurus, senior government officials, journalists and TV producers. Wherever possible it should be added to a business-to-business communications programme.

(b) *Sales promotion* is also a complement to media advertising not a substitute for it. It can carry an advertising message further down the selling line – and can help get fast trial for new product introductions. But its effects are usually short-term, and unless tied firmly to the brand image, its exclusive use can undermine long-term loyalties. It should be used only for what it is good at: for example point-of-sale material, sales force support, dealer incentives, bonuses for customer loyalty.

(c) *Exhibitions and trade fairs* are a powerful tool in the armoury of the business-to-business marketer, although effectiveness varies by product category and by country. They are particularly useful for new product introductions and in fast-growing or new markets. They permit personal contact with potential buyers and give opportunities for 'soft sell' with existing customers. But the costs can be high in terms of numbers of contacts made and the amount of business actually done at the time.

(d) *Direct response* is defined as all advertising and promotion aimed at stimulating immediate action by the customer such as making an enquiry or sending an order to the advertiser. In business-to-business marketing it is usually treated as a part of the advertising rather than as a separate marketing tool. Indeed, the integration of media and direct mail advertising inevitably increases volume of response. And the creation and regular use of a computerised database of customers and prospects is an essential part of most business marketing programmes (see Chapter 16).

FROM A STRATEGY TO A BRIEF

Strategic thinking can be implemented only when it is distilled into a marketing plan, from which a set of briefs can be developed which co-ordinate internal functions, such as production, sales and distribution, with the outside agencies used for advertising, public relations and so on.

The discipline of distilling a marketing plan down to the key points of a brief is the 'acid test' of strategic thinking. This will show up any flaws or missing elements in the thinking. Sound briefing is the only sure foundation on which to develop creative yet relevant advertising and other marketing activity. Most failures can be traced to a brief which was inadequate, misunderstood or not implemented. Advertising makes the link between a customer's need and a supplier's resource. Effective advertising depends on a deep knowledge of both.

The key issues raised so far are all examined in more detail in subsequent chapters.

2

UNDERSTANDING THE DECISION MAKING PROCESS LEADS TO MORE EFFECTIVE ADVERTISING

The philosophy behind all profitable business – know your customers

INTRODUCTION

Important buying decisions, whether business or domestic, are complex and usually taken in stages each of which will involve several people and various sources of influence. One of the keys to success for a supplier of goods and services is to understand this process: who is involved, how they take their decisions, why they make a particular choice and the extent to which it can be affected by advertising and other techniques of communication.

First-hand study of the process and analysis of market research studies have identified a number of common patterns in a variety of business markets. This chapter describes and gives some examples of the most usual of these and suggests from experience how marketing communications can be used most effectively to influence them.

THE TRIGGERS OF BUYER BEHAVIOUR

If a purchase takes place, this means that the buyer has identified a *need*, and has the *opportunity*, *means* and *will* to satisfy it. These we call the 'triggers of buyer behaviour', because if any of them are missing, probably no such purchase will take place.

Unfortunately, in general all four triggers arise from factors beyond the control of any supplier. All the supplier can do about them is to identify (by market or customer research) where and when conditions are right to make a sale.

Traditionally, selling and promotion start at the point when a potential buyer approaches the market by asking for tenders or visiting a showroom. Yet there is much that a customer-orientated supplier can do ahead of time, to make sure that they will be the first (or at least one) of those approached.

A successful marketing strategy will depend on a good understanding of who is concerned with a potential purchase, what steps they will take before deciding, and what input they will need at each stage.

WHO: THE DECISION MAKING UNIT

Almost everybody will take their most trivial purchasing decisions without reference to anyone else, providing the product is for their own consumption or use (such as a snack, a tankful of petrol or an item of office stationery). But if the sum of money involved becomes significant or if the item will be used by other people (or even if others will be aware of its existence), then it is likely that at least one other person will be involved in the purchase. The bigger or more risky the decision, the more people are likely to be consulted. Such a group is called a Decision Making Unit or DMU.

As everyone knows from personal experience, the DMU for consumer products will usually be only the person responsible for making the purchase or the primary family unit of chief wage earner, spouse and sometimes children. More rarely relatives or friends may be consulted on an informal and advisory basis if they are concerned or if there will be repercussions if the choice is wrong.

In businesses, buying decisions are usually more elaborate, with a number of people playing different roles: authorisers, specifiers, specialist advisers, purchasers, users. These are likely to be drawn from different departments, at more than one level of authority or influence, and the bigger the decision the more people become involved. Few may be in a position directly to authorise a purchase, but many (even the most lowly) may have an indirect power of veto over any supplier.

HOW: THE STAGES OF A BUYING DECISION

Figures 2.1–2.4 show examples of how members of business DMUs interact and the sequence which they have to go through. This may be a highly formalised process for a major purchase; it may be much less so for minor or routine decisions except in companies which keep very tight control over expenditure.

Yet in each case before the order is given, the purchaser will have had to identify a need, to search for ways to satisfy it, to budget for the cost and to decide that the end result is worth the trouble and expense. In most cases buyers will have a choice of suppliers, and often the further option of not buying at all. For a 'considered' purchase, this process can go through as many as eight separate and sequential stages.

The eight stages

Stage 1: Identification of need

Nothing happens until someone realises there is a need to be fulfilled. The computerised warehouse system may flag up a shortage of a component. The factory may be having regular trouble with a worn-out machine. A sales executive may be summoned at short notice by a valuable customer. A change in legislation may threaten a company's continued existence.

Stage 2: Decision to search

Private individuals have the luxury of 'looking around' with no commitment, but businesses usually cannot start any action without authorisation, usually from someone at high level, who for the most serious purchases may even demand some kind of feasibility study first.

Stage 3: Determination of specification or requirements

While a private household may or may not wish to consult friends with experience or even outside experts before deciding what to look for, a business will almost always have to produce a written specification for its significant purchases. This will require at the least the input of an internal or external specialist and in some cases consultation with all concerned, perhaps in several departments and levels.

Stage 4: Identification and short-listing of potential suppliers

Information can be gathered by a number of methods: searching directories, reading advertisements, answering coupons, 'asking around', visiting trade fairs, going out to visit showrooms or warehouses, calling in suppliers' representatives, writing for proposals or tenders. The closer to short-list, the more members of the DMU are likely to be consulted – particularly the specifiers and end-users, who may change or add to their requirements as a result.

Stage 5: Final choice and decision to purchase

The most serious step where the 'pros and cons' have to be weighed up carefully. Will the need be fully met? Will it be worth the cost? Can a lower price or better terms be negotiated? Will the supplier be able to fulfil the contract, within the time-frame and with appropriate guarantees in case of trouble? Would an 'optional extra' more or less provide better value?

Stage 6: Final checks

The bigger the decision, the more reassurance the buyer will need before placing the order. Is it within budget? Are there any implications for corporate policy in this purchase or supplier? Could the need be satisfied in any other way? Do we know any other company who has recently bought this, and are they happy about it? How essential is the purchase anyway, could we postpone or abandon the project?

Stage 7: Placing the order

Probably the least stressful part of the process for the buyer, even if not for the supplier!

Stage 8: Following up

After delivery, the buyer will need reassurance that the decision was good, that the product is as specified, and that it does what was wanted by whoever originally identified the need. This feedback will form part of the buyer's collective experience and will be taken into account for future purchases.

Fig. 2.1 A buying sequence: capital equipment by a large firm

1 *Identification of need.* The factory floor – 'Our No. 4 grinder is worn out. Please may we replace?'

2 *Authorisation of search.* Chief Executive – 'Go ahead, within a budget of x.'

3 *Specification.* Engineering – 'We need a machine with a capacity of n units per hour which can accept brass, aluminium and mild steel.'

4 *Search for suppliers.* Purchasing Department – 'Do you wish to tender to this specification?'

5 *Choice.* All the above – 'OK, let's go with this one as the best compromise.'

6 *Authorisation of expenditure & corporate check.* Finance Department – 'Are you within budget?' Specialist adviser – 'Are there any overall corporate implications in this choice?'

7 *The order.* Purchasing – 'We accept your proposal subject to the following.'

8. *Monitoring.* Specifiers and Users – 'Did we get what we want? Is it working properly?'

Fig. 2.2 **A buying sequence: a raw material by a manufacturer**

1 *Identification of need*. Warehouse to Factory manager – 'Stocks of Fastening 469 are down to re-order point.'

2 *Authorisation*. Factory manager to Purchasing manager – 'We need another half-million 469s. Chase them to see they deliver before the end of the month.'

3. *The order*. Purchasing manager to supplier – 'Can you guarantee delivery of 500 boxes of your 469s by end of next week? If so, I will fax our Order.'

4 *Budgeting*. Purchasing to Accounts – 'Purchasing Order no. 123456 to be charged against Small Components.'

5 *Monitoring*. Goods Inward – 'Order no. 123456 just arrived, all complete.'

6 *Follow-up*. All above – 'Our fastenings supplier has given good quality and excellent service all year, we should negotiate with them for next financial year. Is there anything else we could ask them to quote for?'

There are two vital lessons in such a sequence from a marketing point of view. First, that *suppliers will not usually be approached until Stage 4*, by which time a number of key decisions will have been taken (such as the exact specifications). From that point on, the negotiation with potential suppliers will tend to concentrate on price, terms and delivery. Some suppliers might feel they could have been involved to mutual benefit at an earlier stage by suggesting that better options are available on the market.

Second, at all stages, the members of the DMU will have been seeking information of one kind or another about products that might fulfil their needs, their performance and who might supply them. Putting the right information in front of the right people at

Fig. 2.3 A buying sequence: a professional service by a small business

1 *Identification of need*. Company Secretary – 'The Trade Association say that the EU are drafting legislation which will have a big effect on our industry. We need to be properly briefed, but I do not think our local company lawyers are up to this.'

2 *Search for information*. Sales Director – 'My Brussels file has some cuttings about specialist advisers. Shall I write off to the firms mentioned?' MD – 'You do that, and can we all ask around? Sure to be someone at the Golf Club who has had the same trouble.'

3 *Short-listing suppliers*. Company Secretary – 'When I am in London next week, I will call on the firm Charlie's friend spoke highly of and ask how much they would charge to come and talk to us. While I am about it I will go to the one we are all impressed with to see if they look as good face-to-face as their brochure suggests.'

4 *Choice*. MD – 'Are we agreed this firm is the best qualified to help us? They are very expensive but we ought not to economise on such a serious issue.'

6. *Follow-up*. Company Secretary – 'That was a very illuminating presentation. OK if I subscribe to their update service? And will Charlie please keep in touch with the Trade Association so we can get our views known to the lobby.'

the right time might even have got the specification modified to one which only one supplier could fulfil.

Each of the four cases illustrated in Figs. 2.1 to 2.4 shows similarities and differences with the others. They are based on real life, but are not put forward as universal descriptions. For example, Fig. 2.1 describes one way in which a business buys a capital product. But this is not the way every firm buys its machinery, nor how this particular firm buys other goods and services. It will probably buy its raw materials, advertising and pen-

Fig. 2.4 A buying sequence: business travel by a large multinational

1 *Identification of need*. Sales Manager Southern Europe to Personal Assistant – 'Our biggest Italian customer wants to see me on 27th at 10:00. See if you can also fix me a visit to our other customer in Milan the same afternoon so I can come back that night. Then ring the T&T office and ask if there is a sensible morning flight on the 26th. Tell them I do not like our usual hotel there.'

2 *Choice*. Travel & Transport Manager to PA/SMSE – 'Air tickets are on their way to you. I have booked the hotel you said she had to have. It is over Company guidelines so she will need a Director's signature. Does this trip go on the usual Sales Budget number?'

3 *Monitoring*. Accounts Controller to T&T – 'We were well above budget on air travel last quarter. I have asked those responsible to justify. In case this is going to continue can you try for an extra volume discount from our agent?'

sion scheme quite differently. The point is that no supplier can develop a marketing strategy with any chance of success until some such typologies of purchasing behaviour have been identified in the marketplace.

WHY: THE ROLE OF MARKETING COMMUNICATIONS

While these four examples have been chosen to show the breadth of variation, they have certain factors in common. Before a decision to buy is made, all have searched for information, and assessed the value for money of competing products and suppliers against their identified need. All purchases (except perhaps for the most trivial 'impulse purchases') are information-driven.

This information is usually factual, but will often include intangible items such as the reputation of the supplier and the prestige of users among their peer group.

Each of the stages in the process is affected by different factors: the reasons for needing the purchase in the first place are rarely the reasons for choosing supplier A rather than B. The information collected in order to search for a suitable product (its 'specification') will be different from that needed to decide whether or with whom to place the order (the competing suppliers' 'offers' – typically the price, delivery and terms of business). Who is short-listed will depend on who can most closely match the desired specification. Yet frequently no suppliers are approached until this has been decided. It is then relatively hard for a sales team to modify, even if they can offer useful additional product advantages.

It is therefore important for a supplier to make sure that all potential buyers know what they have available at the stage when the need and the kind of product that will satisfy it are still under investigation. The ideal specification from a supplier's point of view will of course be one that is unique to him.

This means that while personal contacts by sales teams or technical representatives are vital to close a sale by negotiation, a relationship needs to have been established with all members of the DMU at a much earlier stage by other less personal means: namely marketing communications.

In the four examples alone, several communications techniques are mentioned or implied: product and corporate image advertising, word-of-mouth, direct mail, print, telephone, sales promotion, public relations, personal presentations. And in these examples, all were effective because they happened to take place at the point they were most relevant and communicated what the decision makers then most needed. If they had come at different times, offered different information or not taken place at all, the buying choice might well have been different too.

PLANNING THE MARKETING COMMUNICATIONS STRATEGY

No effective marketing action can take place until the supplier has taken decisions about the target market, their stages of decision taking, the membership of their DMUs and the information they need at each stage. In some cases, strategic market research will be needed first.

However, given agreed targets, it should then be clear where marketing communications are necessary and what their task is. This will clarify the most appropriate techniques for each stage.

Fig. 2.5 shows that the complete communications task cannot be done by one technique on its own, however much money is spent or however creative its execution. Almost all successful business marketing campaigns integrate several techniques.

For example, *advertising* is excellent at creating among all members of a DMU awareness of a product and its major benefits, reinforcing the reputation of its supplier and reassuring buyers after the event that they have made a wise decision. *Public Relations* activity can reinforce these particularly with specific and influential sub-categories of the target. *Direct Response* can help identify buyers at the time when they are actively searching for information. But to match a product to its potential customers and make the sale itself, *personal contact* will be needed, backed up by literature and interactive techniques such as telephone helplines. By their nature and cost, these techniques must be targeted very narrowly to potential buyers at the point of decision.

Each market will be different, and different suppliers in any market will need different strategies, to the extent that they will be aiming their products at different segments of the total.

For example, although the multinational in Fig. 2.4 buys its executive travel centrally through a specialist travel agent and negotiates special terms by concentrating on one or only a few carriers and hotel chains, these suppliers will be wise to maintain loyalty both by constant personal contact with the decision takers in the Travel and Transport department and by regular media advertising, direct mail and PR aimed at the executive travellers themselves to reassure them that their custom is valued and to ensure that they get the most appropriate service. The opposition will try to find means of undermining this confidence by informing them all of the alternatives on offer.

GENERATING HIGH SALES AT LOW COST

There is no way of generating regular sales without a good product at a price which provides the customer with value for money. But not every such good supplier can have a fair share of a competitive market.

It is essential for high market share to build awareness of the product and its benefits and a good corporate image for its supplier among all decision makers, well ahead of any decisions to buy. Well-known and reliable companies will be approached early in the buying sequence: others may not. Advertising is a highly controllable and low-cost means of achieving this. Only when an interested buyer is in contact with a potential supplier is it sensible to use the highly effective but expensive sale closing techniques such as interactive selling and personal presentation.

Fig. 2.5 How marketing communications can influence a buying decision (example from Fig. 2.1)

Buying sequence	Role of advertising and promotion at each stage	Candidate activity (Marketing/Advertising/Promo)
Stage 1 Identification of need	To highlight the need among target audience – and to demonstrate the problem and the solution	• Advertising • Direct Mail • PR • POS • Cross-selling
Stage 2 Decision to search	To build brand awareness – 'a good company' because of reputation and relevant products	As Stage 1
Stage 3 Requirement or specification	To get on shortlist because product/service meets the perceived need	As Stage 1
Stage 4 Shortlist/Comparison	To build confidence in the company – and to provide all necessary information and assistance	As above plus: • Literature • Personal Advice • Self Help
Stage 5 Decision to purchase	To maintain top-of-mind awareness – and to make decision to purchase simple and attractive	As Stage 4
Stage 6 Checking the decision	To maintain awareness and confidence among target audience and among all possible advisers (professional/informal)	As Stage 4
Stage 7 Purchasing	To make purchase as quick and easy as possible	• Fast friendly response • Simple order/application form • Simple clearance procedure
Stage 8 Did we get what we wanted?	To give reassurance that decision was right – and to build a desire to recommend to others	• Advertising • PR • Follow-up calls

Once the sale is won, advertising and direct mail have useful follow-up roles of reassuring the buyers and pre-selling repeat purchases.

3

WHY WASTE MONEY ON ADVERTISING?

Advertising is a cost unless it sells

THE FUNDAMENTALS OF MARKETING

Money spent on advertising (or any other marketing activity) is a 'cost'. Like all costs it comes straight off 'bottom-line' profits, unless the activity achieves a pre-set objective which improves sales income or margins.

Personal experience or its lack strongly affects each business executive in his or her attitude towards the value and use of advertising. The marketing director who has had a stunning success can have the faith of a new religious convert, while a finance director who has recently seen cash go down the drain trying to rescue a failed new product launch will be fairly cynical. Both are partly right and partly wrong, through being over-influenced by recent and narrowly-based experience.

Yet advertising can and should be measurably effective. A reliable way to achieve this is through the objective study of case histories covering different situations and periods of time so as to distil some general guiding principles about what usually works, and what usually does not. Here are five such experience-based guiding rules, based on over 100 actual cases:

(i) The main cause of success or failure is whether the advertising is developed as an integral part of a *strategically sound marketing plan* or just tacked on as a cosmetic after-thought.

(ii) Strategically sound marketing plans start from the *four fundamentals of marketing* described in Chapter 1:

- the right product at the right price
- the right distribution
- the right relationship with the customers
- the right advertising and promotional mix.

(iii) Successful advertising campaigns have to be of adequate *weight*, appear in the right *media*, and have *creative work* which grabs attention and promises benefits which the customers want or need. If any of these three elements is wrong, it will counteract even the very best work of the others. Over the years they must together present a consistent face for the brand and its supplier (see Chapter 10).

(iv) Effective, measurable advertising should be set an *action standard for success* before any money is spent: 'it will be worth spending this sum of money, provided we get this much extra sales/premium price/new distribution/higher awareness/improved reputation in return.'

(v) You must understand your own company's '*business equation*' and how effective advertising can lever the 'bottom line' upwards.

THE BUSINESS EQUATION

The starting point is to look carefully at the relationship of revenue, costs and profits as sales volume goes up or down. Fig. 3.1 is a simple 'break-even' analysis as used by accountants and marketing economists.

Fig. 3.1 The break-even point

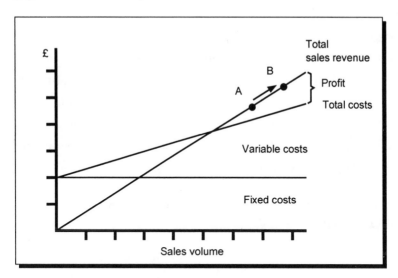

Fixed costs (for example, factory overheads, depreciation of machinery, salaries) are defined as those which remain static within a financial year irrespective of sales volume. *Variable costs* (for example, hourly wages, raw materials, transportation) are those which rise with sales volume. Theory says that unless there are large economies of scale of operations, then the revenue and total costs are straight lines with respect to volume. Where they cross is the 'break-even' point, above which you are in ever-increasing profit.

A simplistic view of advertising might be to assume that its job is to increase the volume of sales so that revenue moves from point A to the more profitable point B. But would it not be better to look for such increased sales volume by means of price cutting?

DO YOUR SUMS BEFORE CUTTING YOUR PRICE

Simple arithmetic can easily demonstrate that price-cutting is the road to destruction. Fig. 3.2 shows how very expensive it is. For example, if your gross profit is 20 per cent, and you cut price by 5 per cent to raise sales, you will need to sell 33 per cent more to make the same amount of gross profit. (There is no magic in this figure, not even a knowledge of accountancy is needed – it can be checked by simple arithmetic.)

Fig. 3.2 The effects of price cutting on profit: how much more volume must you sell to break even?

| | Gross Profit Margin | | | |
	5%	10%	20%	30%
Price Cut				
1%	25	11	5*	3
2%	67	25	11	7
3%	150	43	18	11
5%	–	100	33	20
10%	–	–	100	50

* On a margin of 20%, sales must increase by 5% following a price cut of 1% to maintain the same Gross Profit. This implies a price elasticity of 5.

Price elasticity is an economist's measure of the sensitivity of a market to price, defined as the percentage change in sales volume following a one per cent change in price. If a one per cent price cut raises sales by one per cent the 'coefficient of elasticity' is one. If a one per cent price cut raises sales by more than one per cent, the market is said to be price elastic; if by less than one per cent then the market is said to be inelastic to price.

In this example, for the five per cent cut to be profitable, the elasticity has to be above 33 divided by 5, that is, higher than 6.6.

In reality, few markets show elasticity above 2, and less than 1 is more common.

Therefore unless there is strong evidence to the contrary, price cutting is highly likely to be unprofitable when used as an offensive marketing weapon, even if it succeeds in building sales volume.

THE REALITY OF ADVERTISING

The sales response of a market is usually more complex than this, distorting the textbook 'break-even' position of Fig. 3.1. At low sales volumes, or when demand for a product appears weak, the supplier is under strong psychological pressure to cut prices to customers (or to distributors) to make sure there are at least some sales to contribute to fixed costs. This moves the break-even point to the right.

However, for a product at high volume, or where demand appears to be rising, customers are less reluctant to buy, do not negotiate as hard, and in extreme cases may even buy ahead to guarantee supplies. Consequently, prices firm up, giving the supplier the confidence to take a harder view on cash discounts and other incentives, and switch the tactics to offering extra services for which a premium may even be charged. Fig. 3.3 shows how this 'Wolfe-Armitage' curve increases profitability at higher volumes.

As an illustration of the syndrome, imagine a customer visiting a used car lot at closing time and offering to buy at a discount. If the salesman has not made a sale all day he may well concede, perhaps generously, rather than lose the customer. But after a good day he is more likely to respond with sales talk about the car.

Fig. 3.3 The effect of volume on sales revenue ('Wolfe-Armitage' curve)

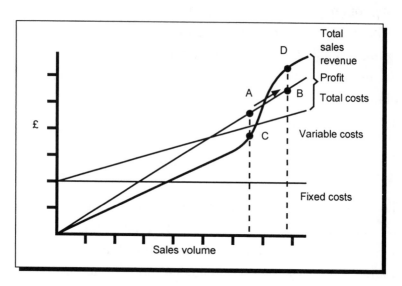

It is therefore highly desirable, not to say profitable, to raise sales well above the theoretical break-even level by means other than price cutting. An advertising campaign, with a carefully defined role and sufficient weight, within a properly developed marketing plan, will work at three separate levels:

(i)   It will motivate the salesforce. They will try to sell more, and at better prices (see Chapter 17).
(ii) It will encourage the distributors to stock more, and then to recommend it to their customers.
(iii) It will encourage the final customers to buy more.

The effect of relatively small gains on each level will multiply, and create major leverage on profits. As Fig. 3.3 shows, successful advertising is likely to move sales income not from A to B, but from C to D. This modest increase in sales volume takes this particular product from below break-even to above, with spectacular effects on the bottom line.

CONCLUSIONS

Successful advertising is likely to be more, not less, cost effective than is generally realised. Indeed if it has *any* positive effect, this is highly likely to be cost-effective in accountancy terms. The opposite is true for price promotions, which are usually less cost effective than is generally believed.

A recent study (reported more fully in Chapter 4) of 1,500 businesses showed that:

- products which are perceived to be of higher quality get higher prices
- there is a direct relationship between this perception of quality and advertising spend
- companies which spend money on advertising at an above average advertising-to-sales ratio, generate a higher ROI than their market competitors.

Price cutting builds volume but not value of sales (unless the market is highly elastic to price). If the market is static (or price-elastic) the first price cutter is likely to touch off a competitive price war, in which product quality and promotional spend have to be sacrificed to fund the price cuts and maintain ROI. This makes the product progressively harder to sell.

Advertising can be used to 'add value' to a product. This increases demand for it, which can be taken by the supplier as either more volume at the same price or the same volume at a higher price. Higher price is harder for the competition to follow, but even where they do a 'premium for quality' war is a benign one for both buyers and sellers.

4

THE IMPACT OF BUSINESS-TO-BUSINESS ADVERTISING ON PROFITS

The companies with the highest Return On Investment have the best quality products – and make sure their customers know it

BACKGROUND

Does it pay marketers to advertise? There is a growing body of hard evidence that advertising can be both effective and cost-effective (particularly the biennial Advertising Effectiveness Awards sponsored by the Institute of Practitioners in Advertising in London, where the winning case histories are published under the title *Advertising Works*). However, most of this relates to consumer goods and services, and the contribution of advertising to profits for business-to-business advertising has been generally harder to document.

A recent study provides important evidence about the way in which advertising drives profitability. It has been carried out on the PIMS (Profit Impact of Marketing Strategy) database, by the Ogilvy Center for Research & Development of San Francisco, California.

THE ANALYSIS OF THE PIMS DATABASE

PIMS has been in existence since the 1960s and is a joint effort of thousands of businesses in the USA and Europe who supply information about their own brands. In exchange, they have the right to analyse the database to generate statistical averages for the database as a whole and by category (confidentiality is kept because data relating to individual firms cannot be isolated). The Strategic Planning Institute of Cambridge, Massachusetts, was formed in 1975 by the participating businesses to manage the database and to facilitate the analyses.

Most of the analyses are done by participating firms for their own benefit, but occasionally an analysis has been published (for example, in *Harvard Business Review*).

Over 1,500 of the firms in PIMS are classified as operating in the business-to-business sector, and this analysis relates to them alone. They were further sub-categorised in terms of the amount of money they spent on advertising their brands in relation to their competition: namely into five groups whose advertising-to-sales ratios (A:S) compared with market average were much higher, higher, equal, lower and much lower. These five groups were then compared over a range of other characteristics contained in PIMS.

THE FINDINGS

1: Advertising affects perception of quality

All brands were classified in terms of their customers' perceptions of their quality. These 'perceived quality' scores are comparative with competitors in the same market. The evaluation is derived directly from market research or through management's best estimates of customer perception.

It was found that brands seen as being of relatively higher quality achieve prices that average seven per cent higher than competition. The businesses that produce them realise an average ROI of 29 per cent, while businesses whose brands were seen as relatively low in quality only managed to achieve an average ROI of 16 per cent.

Fig. 4.1 compares the customers' perceived quality ratings against advertising-to-sales ratios. There is a clear positive correlation between perception of quality and advertising pressure. Indeed, brands with the highest A:S ratios gain product quality scores 45 per cent higher than those who do not advertise at all.

Fig. 4.1 Relationship of advertising spending to perceived product quality

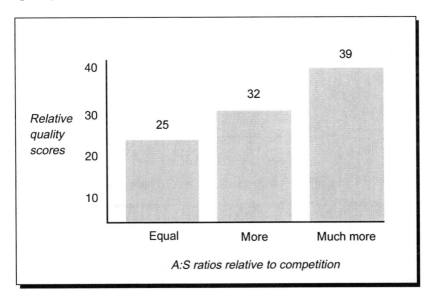

While it might be tempting to deduce that heavy advertising could be used to compensate for mediocre quality, PIMS data clearly demonstrate that this is not the case. But when product quality is genuinely high, advertising can reinforce and amplify this perception.

2: Relative advertising pressure and market share are related

The five A:S ratio categories were compared in terms of their share of market. Brands with low A:S ratios operate at substantially lower shares of market than ones with higher A:S ratios.

Fig. 4.2 Relationship of A:S ratios and market share

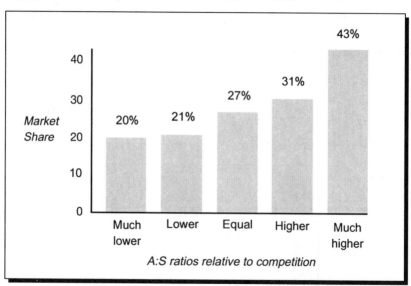

3: Return On Investment is strongly related to market share

When market shares were cross-analysed by Return On Investment, it appeared (not surprisingly) that brands with relatively high shares earned an average return that was twice as high as brands with low shares.

Fig. 4.3 ROI & relative market share

Share level	ROI
HIGH	30%
MEDIUM	22%
LOW	15%

It must not be assumed from Fig. 4.3 that increasing market share will automatically increase ROI. Brands which are successful (in terms of achieving a high ROI) are likely to have achieved high shares of their market, but the correlation does not necessarily work both ways. Companies that attempt share building strategies single-mindedly in bad years as in good soon find that competitors are forced to retaliate, and that consequently their margins are squeezed.

4: Businesses which invest in advertising obtain higher ROIs

Since the relative level of a business's advertising investment and its share of market are related, and since share is related to ROI, it follows that there should be a relationship between advertising spending and profits.

To study this, brands which were and were not advertised were compared with the expected average ROI. This 'expected average' was based on a profitability model which took into account a range of other factors that affected profits.

The analysis showed that firms which employ advertising as one of their marketing techniques obtain an ROI on their brands which is on average 14 per cent higher than that of non-advertisers.

5: Higher A:S ratios are directly related to higher ROIs

Evidence of this relationship comes from a separate analysis of relative advertising-to-sales ratios.

Fig. 4.4 Relationship of comparative A:S ratios to ROI

A:S ratio compared with competitors	Average ROI
Much higher	32%
Higher	25%
Equal	24%
Lower	19%
Much lower	20%

This confirms that there is a positive correlation between advertising spend and ROI; brands with higher A:S ratios enjoying increasingly attractive ROIs.

SUMMARY

An analysis of more than 1,500 businesses in Europe and the USA documented in the PIMS database and who operate in the business-to-business sector gives consistent evidence that firms which advertise their brands achieve a better perception of product quality among their customers, hold higher shares of their market and above all gain a 14 per cent higher ROI than those which do not.

Further:

- brands seen as being of higher quality than their competition command higher prices
- perceptions of higher quality are related to higher advertising-to-sales ratios
- brands with higher advertising-to-sales ratios achieve a higher share of market
- the brands which have the highest return on investment are also the brands with the highest relative advertising-to-sales ratios.

As with all such analyses, the caution must be made that while the correlations are statistically valid, they do not on their own imply direct causation in either direction. In particular, the findings do not imply that spending more money on advertising on its own will automatically result in a better image for quality, higher market share or above-average ROI.

Almost certainly, the companies with the highest ROI are successful not just because they advertise but because advertising is a visible indicator of an above-average strategic marketing effort. The PIMS database does not contain the information to prove this, but it is highly likely that these companies also spend above-average amounts on market research, new product development, good customer contact and a wide range of other marketing communications with their customers and prospects. Advertising is an essential but not unique part of their strategy which they have in common.

5

SETTING A BUDGET AND ALLOCATING RESOURCES

How much should I spend? The hardest question facing any advertiser

ADVERTISING MUST PAY FOR ITSELF

The effectiveness of a campaign depends on the amount of money spent, the efficiency of the media plan in putting the message in front of its target market and the originality of its content. These three elements are all vital and dependent on each other in the sense that a weakness in one will cancel out success elsewhere. This chapter deals with the first element: the advertising budget.

This book everywhere reinforces its motto: 'advertising is a cost unless it sells'. This belief in the fundamental necessity of 'accountability' leads to a clear viewpoint on the approach and techniques available to aid the setting of budgets, for advertising, for other marketing activity and indeed for any form of business expenditure.

Experience teaches that:

(i) there is no universal mechanical approach which can replace a *proper business judgement* based on good external market intelligence and good internal financial systems which together give a full understanding of the company's dynamics. When allocating money, advertising should not be treated differently from any other form of expenditure.

(ii)   no solution can be right unless it balances the two opposing views summarised in Chapter 3:

- the expansionist approach of marketing management who believe in the necessity to spend money to drive up sales and market share
- the cautious views of financial management who wish to protect margins by controlling costs, and who see advertising as an expense threatening the 'bottom line' which should be minimised.

(iii) the point of reconciliation is to agree quantified *action standards* before setting a budget which commits money to any activity. The key question is to know the effect on final profits of achieving or failing to achieve the action standards.

(iv) questions of target sales volume and value (that is, prices) must be accurately and fully answered. As shown in Chapter 3 any change in customer demand can affect prices and margins as well as sales volume. So advertising can be used to help in the recovery of 'fixed overhead costs' at lower sales levels, or lower the break-even point through higher prices, or build profits through higher sales volume when above break-even point.

(v)   in many situations, a 'profit analysis' of alternative scenarios with different levels of sales and advertising budgets, leading to 'action standards' for success, will provide a valuable basis for identifying strategies most likely to provide outcomes which are both desirable and practicable. For example, in years of heavy competition, achieved price is likely to drift below target. As shown in Chapters 3 and 4, advertising can be set the objective of firming it up.

(vi) the rest is experience, knowledge of the competitive market situation, and a hard-nosed and persistent attitude to campaign evaluation.

HOW ARE BUDGETS SET IN PRACTICE?

There are a number of techniques which are in regular use by companies to set their budget for advertising. Fig. 5.1 lists the most common of them. They can be classified under three headings:

(i)   pragmatic methods
(ii) task-orientated methods
(iii) analytic and experimental methods.

In practice, increasing numbers of business-to-business advertisers claim to base their budgets on pre-determined advertising-to-sales ratios, or various forms of task-orientated methods. Unfortunately these methods often beg the key questions: how were the ratios derived in the first place? Why match competition if they are over-spending? If we believe market conditions have changed, will last year's formula still hold?

Others claim to take a more intuitive view, based on previous experience and market 'feel'. There is no substitute for first-hand experience, and indeed if there is no other basis on which to take any decision it is commonsense to take the views of the most knowledgeable. But such intuitive systems cannot be studied or learned by somebody else, and when they go wrong provide no basis on which to correct their errors.

If advertising is to be accountable, it must be based on an analytic approach using as much market research and management information as possible. A logical, quantified and documented approach will provide top management with a basis for

Fig. 5.1   Methods of setting advertising budgets

Pragmatic methods

1   a pre-determined advertising-to-sales ratio (percentage of sales at ex-factory price or a fixed sum per unit).

2   a 'residual' after deducting from gross margins required net profit, and costs deemed to have higher priority.

3   dominating, matching or otherwise relating to competitors' expected expenditures.

4   maintaining previous years' levels, taking into account inflation of media costs.

Task-oriented methods

Estimating the cost of achieving tasks which advertising could be expected to carry out, e.g:

5   pre-determined investment per head per customer.

6   pre-determined numbers of impacts per head on customers or potentials.

7   calculating the marginal revenue needed to justify a marginal increase in expenditure.

8   matching share of advertising to desired share of market.

9   matching changes in advertising to changes in sales volume or share.

Analytic and experimental methods

10   simple *models* of the marketing process relating advertising levels to absolute or relative changes in volume or share.

11   more sophisticated *dynamic models*, such as *econometrics*, based on past patterns of changes in sales related to key variables in the market such as economic conditions, price, advertising and competition.

12   *marketing experiments.* Advertising expenditure and media plans generally vary over time for a variety of reasons. The results of these variations can be studied analytically, as suggested in 11. The likelihood of gaining actionable information is improved if the breadth of variation is increased artificially and on a controlled basis by medium, by market segment or by region. The usual technique is 'weight-testing', where all other marketing variables except advertising weight are kept constant throughout the country, but different pressures of advertising are applied in different areas or in different media.

achieving a balance between over-expansionism in the Marketing Department and over-caution in the Finance Department, and will encourage both to learn by experience. The reason for their difference may well be a lack of understanding of the 'business equation' described in Chapter 3, and the financial dynamics which link the company's resources with the needs of the market.

A RECOMMENDED APPROACH

As part of the annual planning process, the Marketing Director should go through the following steps:

(i)   What is the task? (Marketing Management's quantified sales targets and the specific role of advertising in achieving them.)

(ii) What is it worth us spending to achieve that? (The views of the Financial Department.)

(iii) How should we best use that sum? (Recommendations and plans from the agency.)

(iv) Will that work in practice? (Joint discussion based on analysis of past experience and judgement.)

If the answer to question (iv) is 'yes', then the recommended budget can be set with confidence that it will be appropriate for the target. If not, then the sequence has to be repeated with adjusted targets and plans until a realistic budget is reached. Obviously, question (iv) is the most difficult. A view of the success or otherwise of the past can be built up from a regular set of action-standards and evaluative measures which are carefully monitored. This will help to make sure that the decision is improved year on year (see Chapter 12).

Consistency is important. Massive spending in one year with

nothing to follow will be less effective than the same total amount divided and spread over two to three years. To set over-optimistic goals with inevitable cutbacks at mid-year or from year to year will interrupt communications with the customers, and demoralise the marketing and sales staff. It is always better to set sales targets at achievable levels. Any opportunity to exceed target sales can then easily be funded, and those responsible well rewarded for their success. Companies whose objectives and budgets are set realistically (and who therefore regularly exceed sales targets) are well motivated and attractive places to work.

6

THE IMPORTANCE OF CORPORATE IMAGE

The business buyer wants to know not just 'What Product?' but 'Whose Product?'

THE NEED FOR A GOOD REPUTATION

One of the longest-running successful business-to-business advertisements is by McGraw-Hill's trade magazines. It shows a stern-faced businessman in his office chair saying:

> *I don't know your company.*
>
> *I don't know your company's product.*
>
> *I don't know what your company stands for.*
>
> *I don't know your company's record.*
>
> *I don't know your company's reputation.*
>
> *Now what was it you wanted to sell me?*

The message is clear. Of course a product has to offer the right specification, at the right price, with the appropriate terms for delivery and after-sales service. But before committing company funds, a business buyer will also need reassurance on the bona fides of the seller: his reputation for fair dealing, financial stability, and so on. Could problems arise in dealing with this company: such as frequent stoppages by a discontented workforce, poor quality control, or ownership in a politically embarrassing country?

This advertisement first appeared in the 1930s. Half-a-century on there are extra problems. Companies selling to businesses are increasingly aware that besides their present and potential customers, they must also preserve a good reputation among a number of people *who do not buy the product.*

'NON-CUSTOMER' PUBLICS

These extra target publics include any person or organisation who can help or hinder the company in its efforts to achieve its long-term objectives. They are typified in Fig. 6.1. Such people may never need to buy the company's products, but still have the power to cause it problems and divert resources (and the attention of those in charge) away from its selling effort.

Companies should also consider their own *employees* as a 'public' of prime concern, particularly large organisations with huge and scattered workforces, all of whom 'represent' the company to their friends and neighbours, as well as to their external contacts for business purposes. Indeed, it can be argued that the importance of good internal communication in building the reputation of a company is often under-estimated (see Chapter 17).

REPUTATION MANAGEMENT

No vital matters can be left to chance, and a wise company man-

Fig. 6.1 Examples of 'non-customer' publics

- Central and local government
- Political activists and pressure groups
- Trade Unions
- Opinion formers
- The media
- The financial community
- University and school teachers
- Graduates and school-leavers
- Local residents

ages its corporate reputation with as much care as any other part of its operations.

Reputation management is a continuous process. Every company is continually at risk from a range of perils: natural disasters, human error, financial and media predators, even international criminals. Only some of the risks can be anticipated or insured against; for the rest, to wait until trouble strikes is far too late. An embittered strike, an accidental pollution of the river, a corporate raid, an 'investigative' TV programme, an adverse medical report on a major ingredient, a terrorist's threat, even a spectacular divorce by a key employee, can have sudden adverse effects on sales or on a company's rating as an investment or employer. The victimised company will wish to exonerate itself, or at least put its point of view. Yet efforts at such a time are likely to be seen as 'special pleading' and can even reinforce the accusations they are intended to rebut: 'no smoke without fire!', or 'they would say that wouldn't they!'

Fig. 6.2 Potential corporate threats

- Financial predators
- 'Investigative' media
- Interventionist governments (local, central, trans-national)
- Militant environmentalists/consumerists
- Terrorists, criminals
- Employee errors, frauds, scandals
- Natural disasters, accidents, failures

The fundamental step to building and protecting a good reputation is to carry out regular tracking of corporate image among buying and non-buying publics, to detect potential weaknesses early, and to confirm existing strengths. Research is invaluable because what a company may be most proud of, or regard as an asset, may be seen in a different light by the public, or even as totally irrelevant. This can also work the other way: companies initiating a major up-date have sometimes discovered that what they denigrated as 'old-fashioned' was highly regarded by their customers and the financial community as evidence of sound reliability!

Strategies for modifying corporate reputations have to be laid for the long term, because while it is easy to reinforce positive attitudes, it takes time to add new ideas, and even longer to overcome prejudices and reverse negative views.

The best (and essential) generator of a good corporate image is good corporate behaviour: high and consistent quality products, regular improvements and innovations, good value for money, fair dealing with customers, prompt and courteous handling of enquiries and complaints, well qualified, trained and motivated staff, good and consistently executed policies for dealings with government, local communities and the environment. If any of these is seriously wrong, no amount of promotion of the company can put it right on its own, and it could (by highlighting the weaknesses) be counter-productive.

PROMOTING THE COMPANY AND ITS PRODUCTS

Yet in a highly competitive world, doing a good job is unfortunately insufficient. Positive action has to be taken to promote both product and producer. Fig. 6.3 offers a wide choice of techniques.

Fig. 6.3 Techniques for corporate communication

- Livery, house style, stationery
- Packaging and literature
- Premises and vehicles
- Media advertising
- Direct mail
- Public relations
- Sponsorship of sports and arts
- Local events
- Trade fairs and conferences
- Sales promotions
- In-house videos and news-sheets

Many of these will be in use already for promoting brands or ranges of products, but such activity will be designed to specific briefs and aimed at narrow targets. The general public may see a variety of such material, so it is important that it all shows consistency in corporate matters, and reinforces the desired reputation. Everyone concerned with promoting the products must therefore be made aware of corporate requirements.

BUILDING A CORPORATE IMAGE

On top of that, and separate from all efforts designed to build sales, it is strongly advisable to open a channel of communication directly with relevant non-buying publics, and even the public at large, through a 'corporate image' campaign of media advertising and public relations.

Such activity is ideally started in 'good' times, so that it can begin by reinforcing the most widely accepted positive and informative aspects of the company. Only when this channel is recognised and accepted as reliable by its audiences should more controversial communications be attempted, such as correction of prejudices or the introduction of new or unknown facts. For example, the oil industry is particularly vulnerable to attack. Shell have shown admirable consistency in their corporate communications, by promoting themselves as the motorist's friend since the 1930s using the slogan 'You can be sure of Shell'. More recently this same slogan has been used successfully in putting a case about environmental pollution.

CHOICE OF MEDIA

It is highly likely that a variety of techniques will be needed. For example, some target populations will be small in numbers and known by name or at least by job titles (such as MPs or Pension Fund Managers) making *Direct Mail and PR* highly cost-effective. Carefully chosen *sponsorships* can sometimes make a subtle statement in an acceptable way that a company cares about its local community, or does not damage the environment, or has high cultural standards.

All *staff* who contact the public have daily chances to do good (or harm) and so need training and back-up material. The sales-force, obviously, but the staff at the switchboard, reception, gate-keepers, and the staff at the enquiries counter also deserve special attention. And any customer (or journalist) forced to follow for miles behind a filthy and inconsiderately driven delivery van is likely to put its owner on a personal hit-list!

But all these should be seen as *supporting* activity, and usually need to be spearheaded by *media advertising*. Unlike almost all 'below-the-line' techniques, this is totally controllable in terms of who sees what, where, when, and at what frequency.

Contrary to expectations, this need not be expensive. *Once established*, a favourable corporate image can be maintained by a regular modest strategic 'holding' weight, to be reinforced for tactical offensive or defensive purposes only whenever circumstances demand. Such tactical bursts can be mounted at short notice, yet be accepted as part of the established programme. (Compare the adverse reactions to some unexpected and over-weight efforts by some of the nationalised industries in Britain during their privatisation programmes!)

CHOICE OF CONTENT

There is no question that much 'corporate advertising' is wasted, or even counter-productive, because it 'massages the corporate ego' by concentrating on aspects of interest and pride to the company's management to the exclusion of what the audience wants to know or worries about. Morale building is a legitimate exercise, but there are usually cheaper ways of motivating staff than national media! Research is a better discipline for identifying salient and above all *relevant* issues.

As the 'official' face of the company, corporate advertising must look *important* in its size, positioning and style. Its tone of voice must match the corporate objectives. The presentation itself must be *credible, single-minded, consistent,* and as *involving* to the audience as possible. A flexible but recognisable framework will aid the introduction of new topics in a hurry.

It should offer a chance to respond (by sending in a coupon, ringing a number, entering a competition, writing for a booklet or video). This is a good way of defusing resentment, building up mailing lists of concerned friends and getting to know the enemy at first hand.

INTERNAL COMMUNICATIONS

Top management must be involved with, and supportive of, such corporate activity from the beginning. It is not putting the case too strongly to suggest that where the product to be promoted is the company itself, the 'brand manager' should be the Chief Executive.

Before launch, the campaign should be 'merchandised' to the whole staff: by personal presentation, video, newsletter (see

Chapter 17). Top management should be seen to be involved, and should underline the importance of corporate image. This ensures consistent reinforcement throughout the company.

The benefits are widespread:

- better management-to-staff relationships
- higher staff morale and pride
- consistency of communication with the outside world
- motivation of sales forces.

Fig. 6.4 The 10 'golden rules' for maintaining a favourable corporate image

1　Start communicating early

2　Research before planning

3　Involve top management

4　Set clearly defined, specific, realistic goals

5　Be relevant to the chosen audience

6　Be credible, single-minded, consistent, involving

7　Create an important-looking, recognisable, flexible style

8　Offer a chance to respond

9　Merchandise the campaign to the whole workforce

10　Measure results

CONCLUSION

A good corporate reputation is an asset to a company on which an actual cash value can be put in the balance sheet, namely 'goodwill'.

Corporate advertising is one of the strategic weapons available to build that reputation, and then guard it against the continual risk of misfortune or enemy attack.

A corporate campaign does not 'sell' anything (except perhaps incidentally). But it generates climates of opinion (both outside and inside the company) within which the company's marketing effort can be carried on for maximum effect and with the minimum of hindrance.

The creation of a successful corporate campaign does not differ *in principle* from other types of advertising: realistic, research-based objectives have to be set, specific target audiences selected, creative material pre-tested, supporting material chosen and co-ordinated, results tracked.

However, successful corporate advertising demands a consistent corporate resolve. Like growing asparagus, one needs to start at least three years ahead of the desired results; so the corporate reputation must be on the agenda for all senior management *now*.

7

PUTTING IT ALL TOGETHER

*How to make the most of the marketing communications budget in
business-to-business marketing*

THE ROLE OF MARKETING COMMUNICATIONS

Everyone who sells goods or services to businesses (as opposed
to domestic consumers) knows that personal contact is the best
selling technique, that word-of-mouth is the most powerful
advertising medium, and that a good product offering fair value
for money is the best route to repeat purchasing.

But how does a business induce potential customers to try the
good product in the first place? How does it keep a strong and
favourable image in the face of heavy competition? Unsupported
personal contact is too expensive to permit regular cold canvass-
ing (now costing over £200 per call in Britain, and more in most
other European countries, according to McGraw-Hill; see Chapter 18). Word-of-mouth is very slow and uncertain in its growth,
and has to be seeded to be relied upon.

Such support and seeding are conventionally done by marketing communications, with the intention of creating awareness,
supplying information, building favourable images and attitudes,
generating response, and preparing for and following up visits by
the salesforce. Marketers have a wide choice of possible promotional techniques, particularly: media advertising, print, mail and
other direct response, sales force aids, sales promotion, trade
fairs, public relations, sponsorship.

There is much evidence from both consumer and business markets that such activity (if done creatively and at the right level) can be not only effective in building profitable sales but also highly cost-effective, particularly in comparison with more primitive tactics such as price cutting (see Chapter 3).

But how can a business-to-business marketer choose the most appropriate marketing communications (marcoms)? How should a budget be allocated between them? How can the different parts of the promotional mix be integrated to reinforce each other, and carry out their specific yet possibly different tasks?

THE CONTRAST BETWEEN BUSINESS AND CONSUMER MARKETING

These problems are less acute in consumer goods. Because many such markets are large enough to contain relatively homogeneous target segments suitable for mass-marketing, most advertising and promotional media are well researched on an industry basis. Key tasks are easy to identify (such as placating a dominant distribution chain), and the marketing budget is a large enough percentage of total costs to justify market research to fill gaps in the database and to buy into syndicated tracking studies to evaluate and fine-tune response.

Many product managers in packaged goods appear to have simplified their marcom strategies down to offering large promotional discounts to 'key account' retailers, with television advertising in support at a weight as heavy as the rest of the budget will buy. They regard any additional activity as a token luxury for use in good years!

The choice of promotional techniques has to be decided differently in business markets. A high proportion of sales usually comes from a small number of large buyers who often differ significantly from each other in their needs and methods of doing business. The choice of relevant advertising media is usually limited and easily saturated.

Economical syndicated facilities for market, media and tracking research are not usually available, and even market leaders can rarely justify large research programmes out of their promotional budgets. Many companies face such problems, and this chapter offers some approaches based on experience.

THE STARTING POINT – CLEAR OBJECTIVES

As stated in the Introduction, the starting point for any successful marketing activity must be an agreed statement of *Marketing Objectives* developed from the company's long-term Business Plan and consequently integrated with the company's other activities. These Objectives should make clear what kind and size of company we wish to be, where we want to be positioned in the marketplace, who we intend should buy our product and how we want them to regard us.

Companies who keep good sales records know the names and addresses of all their target customers, and can specify about each a number of facts, such as size, industry, end-use of the product and whether they are regular, occasional, lapsed or non-buyers. Many also keep records of members of the relevant DMU in each customer by job-function (authorisers, specifiers, specialist advisers, buyers, users) and even by name.

Not so many are aware of the importance to the success of the company of a number of other people and institutions who are therefore also possible targets for regular communication. For example, suppliers and distributors, the financial community, the media, opinion leaders, Government, political and other pressure groups, local communities where plant is located, and the company workforce – particularly those located far from Head Office.

Some of these people can be of direct and positive help to the marketing effort but, more importantly, many of them are in a position to hinder. Part of the corporate communications programme must therefore be designed to supply these groups with information which is useful to them and which reinforces the good reputation of the company (see Chapter 6).

THE COMMUNICATIONS AUDIT

Once the business and marketing objectives and the potential customer and non-customer target groups have been identified, it is useful to carry out a *communications audit*. This can be done in-house but there may be advantages in using an outside expert who will be familiar with the method and more objective in reporting.

Such an audit reviews all communication channels which have been used in the past, recording the materials, content, styles, frequency and cost. It should cover all external and internal communication methods likely to have been seen by any of the target groups. For example, all print material such as news-sheets, price lists and sales letters, media advertising, presentations, stands at trade fairs, sales aids, promotions and PR used for sales support, and everything subject to house styling such as product packaging, stationery and vehicles. Also all personal contacts with outsiders, not only by sales people but also by reception, telephone, service and repair staff; how are they briefed, are they expected to give feed-back?

Next the audit should look at each of the target groups. To how much of this activity and from which sources will they have been exposed? What is the degree of overlap? What messages will have been communicated? Did they respond and in what way? What is our company's reputation on key dimensions? How does all of that compare with competitors and their activities?

While exposure data may be available from some media and certain response data should be collected routinely in-house, it will be necessary to gather much of this information directly from samples of the target markets themselves. Such research may well repay part of its costs by acting later as a baseline for tracking the effects of subsequent activity.

Fig. 7.1 Examples of problems uncovered by communications audit

- Mixed identities in markets
- Lack of establishment of brand qualities
- No central collation of information
- Out-dated positioning of company
- Poor application of identity
- Lack of staff appreciation of company goals

Analysis and reporting on all this information will show up the basic strengths and weaknesses in the communications mix of our company and its competitors. It can help to determine the extent to which the set communication objectives have been achieved, which targets have been neglected or over-exposed, where money is being wasted, which techniques have been most effective, which messages have been accepted and where there have been misunderstandings or conflicts.

MATCHING THE MESSAGE TO THE TARGETS

The Statement of Objectives usually makes clear which messages ought to be communicated to all targets (for example a common corporate image) and which must be kept specific to small groups (for example, sampling promotions to new buyers only, technical financial data to major institutional investors only).

A useful planning aid at this point is a grid listing the messages to be communicated and the targets to which they should (and ideally should not) be addressed. This will point out where wide and narrow communications media will be most needed.

Fig 7.2 A campaign planning grid

	Customers	Prospects	Suppliers	Opinion formers, media	Government, pressure groups	Financial institutions	Local communities	Employees
Good corporate image	●	●	●	●	●	●	●	●
High quality product	●	●		●				●
Good service	●	●						●
Terms of business	●	●	●					●
Financially sound					●	●		●
Good employer, good neighbour				●	●		●	●

MATCHING THE MESSAGE TO THE TARGET –
HOW TO CHOOSE MARCOMS TECHNIQUES

If an agency specialising in marketing communications has not already been employed to conduct the audit, one should be brought in now to help to short-list the most appropriate vehicles or techniques. What are the methods available for reaching each of the targets? How much do they cost, and what can be obtained for the money? Which of them are best for putting across each of the desired messages?

These are specialised questions, and need professional answers. From the short-list, agency and client should make final choices together.

Fig. 7.3 Markets, tasks and media

Market	Communications task	Media

Customers
  existing
 	
  potential
	create loyalty
	cross-sell
	attract leads,
	new business
		direct mail
		
		advertising, PR
		direct mail

Intermediaries/ distributors	maintain customer contact tie-in key referral points	advertising, PR, sponsorship
Influencers	put company case	advertising, PR
Suppliers	tie-in	direct mail, sponsorship
Employees	brief on company objectives, reinforce loyalty	meetings, newsletters, sponsorship

Criteria for judging include the budget available for spending on each target, the expected market environment and competitive climate, the apparent effects of past activity as revealed by the audit, the likely overlap between methods and their relative suitability for the recommended creative approach. (For example, if the best-selling point of a machine is its effectiveness or ease of use, then expensive film, video and personal demonstrations are of higher priority over more economical print. If the comparative advantage concerns good maintenance and low installation costs, the decision may be the other way.)

Most business-to-business marketing problems need a combination of techniques to solve them cost-effectively and a trade-off between alternative choices of promotional mix will usually be necessary.

SETTING THE PROMOTIONAL BUDGET

Sometimes the set budget may not appear sufficient to achieve all the tasks successfully. In such a case both the budget and the tasks should be reviewed carefully to see whether the targets have been set unrealistically high or whether too much money has been directed into activities of a lower priority (see Chapter 5).

If, as a result of such a review, further funds cannot be found elsewhere, the advertiser is recommended to concentrate efforts on fewer tasks aimed at the targets with highest priority. Experience shows that fragmentation of effort wastes money yet, conversely, highly successful activity aimed directly against one objective will often have a 'halo effect' over some of the others.

For example, Chapter 4 showed that customers will pay premium prices to suppliers they believe to have higher-quality products. Hence, improving quality and informing the customers is usually a more profitable use of marketing funds than cutting price.

THE IMPORTANCE OF A GOOD CORPORATE IMAGE

The common element in all communications is the corporate image of their originator. Most of the target groups, intentionally or not, will be exposed to more than one source of information. Customers' managements probably read the financial press, some MPs or newspaper reporters may live near your factory. It is important that all intended messages reinforce each other, and that inadvertent ones do not create conflict, otherwise the effectiveness of all activity will be undermined.

For example, users' perceptions of the (genuine) high quality of a product may be devalued if it is packed in low-grade, badly printed card and delivered by a vehicle which appears not to have been washed or serviced in months. Those companies who were widely reported to have (however justifiably) given top management unprecedented salary increases in a recession year lost credibility both with their workforce as good employers and with investors as responsible strategic managers of people and funds.

Hence the desired elements of the corporate image and house styling must be specified, widely circulated, and made mandatory for all external communications and activities which impinge on the outside world.

Indeed a special 'image' advertising campaign may be a cost-effective way of simultaneously covering some of the non-customer target groups and of reinforcing harder-pointed promotional activity aimed at customers.

THE COMMUNICATIONS MIX

The need to use a combination of techniques is a strength rather than a weakness of business-to-business campaigns. It means that the creative approach can be fine-tuned to the nature of each medium and its relationship to its audience, which is not usually possible with the 'shot-gun' techniques of mass consumer campaigns. Costs can be minimised by planning source material such as photography and video with the whole range of end-uses in mind.

Secondly, research has shown that campaigns which combine approaches are usually more effective than those putting the whole budget behind a single communication technique. For example, direct mail shots consistently pull higher response if pre-sold by advertising in the relevant media. Sales forces get a better reception if calls are preceded by a personalised mailing (see Chapter 15).

Sponsorship of sports or arts is usually a waste of money if used on its own. The unadorned appearance of a relatively unknown name on an opera programme, cricket boundary or runner's number cloth will suggest nothing to the spectator.

Yet sponsorship can be a very cost-effective way of supporting an image, if carefully chosen to reinforce the main campaign theme (for example, high technology, care for the environment, traditionalism, perhaps even the product's performance under gruelling conditions). A sponsored event also offers opportunities for the entertainment and tactful pressurising of customers, media and influential opinion formers.

PUTTING IT ALL TOGETHER

In the 1990s and onwards, business-to-business markets may well provide better opportunities for good creativity and sound commercial judgement than consumer markets, where in many cases changing circumstances have forced competitors into a choice between 'look-alike' mainstream solutions and highly original irrelevance.

For those who have depth of knowledge and first-hand experience of the wide range of options open to business marketers, there are good opportunities to run original, cost-effective, integrated, multi-technique campaigns. Sometimes there is still the chance to pre-empt the high ground, leaving the competition the choice of keeping away or appearing a 'me-too'.

Fig. 7.4 Six 'golden rules' for success

1 Plan on the basis of fact: audit the resources and research the customers

2 Set specific marketing objectives arising from the corporate business plan

3 Define communication targets (both customer and non-customer)

4 Set and enforce common elements of corporate image and house style

5 Be consistent over time and across techniques

6 Seek the advice of specialists who are qualified to plan and execute over a wide range of techniques, and who have depth of experience in business rather than consumer markets.

The main counter-threats to guard against are those of fragmentation of effort, irrelevance and inconsistency. The potential rewards of success are immediate improvements in the cost-effectiveness of the marketing budget, growing synergy of marketing with other activities, and the long-term stability of profit margins enjoyed by companies with the highest reputation.

Part B

EXECUTING
AND EVALUATING
A CAMPAIGN

8

CREATIVITY: WHAT WORKS – AND HOW TO GET IT FROM YOUR AGENCY

Creativity is not the icing on the cake, it is the self-raising agent which makes it edible

THE FIVE GOLDEN RULES OF SUCCESSFUL ADVERTISING

This chapter was originally written by the Creative Director of an agency. It summarises from his first-hand experience and a great deal of research, why some advertising works, and some does not; and lists reasons why even an agency with a reputation for success may still on occasion produce the opposite. It offers advertisers some guidelines on how to distinguish successful creative work from potential failure, and how to improve the chances of getting it from an agency.

The sub-heading above may seem inappropriate. Surely advertising is an industry where creativity, originality and innovation mean everything? How can there be rules? In fact, as research helps to demonstrate, there are five basic principles that ensure effective, focussed creativity. They are the criteria by which good creative departments judge their work. Despite their simplicity, and indeed manifest good sense, a great deal of business-to-business advertising appears to break them, most of the time and for no apparent good reasons. An effective advertisement may sometimes break *one*, but only for a good, and thoroughly debated reason.

A successful advertisement must:

(i)   grab the attention of its target
(ii) be relevant to the product and its buyers and users
(iii) be clearly and uniquely branded
(iv) be consistent from showing to showing and year to year
(v)   promise a benefit.

These are the necessary minimum criteria for success in that any advertisement missing all or most of them is likely to be a waste of money; but in advertising there are no guarantees for success even for well-behaved advertisements! Yet more than this is necessary – namely creativity.

WHAT MAKES ADVERTISING WORK?

Research also provides clues about specific 'dos and don'ts'. The following list of 20 points is by no means exhaustive, but sets out some of the established facts about advertising:

1 Many of the successful techniques of consumer advertising work in business-to-business: promising a benefit, news, testimonials, recognising a problem, giving helpful information, and so on.

2 Advertisements must be able to communicate extremely quickly (if not their whole message, at least something meaningful and useful). The average reader looks at an advertisement for an average of 2.5 seconds and then passes on unless something in it has encouraged him or her to stay longer. People do not pause to decode ads which have no immediate meaning for

Fig. 8.1 The five 'Golden Rules' for successful advertising

1 An advertisement cannot even start to do its job unless it *gains attention* from its target audience. Successful advertising is highly visible, and stands out probably because it is different. Invisible, 'me-too', advertising clichés must be a waste of money.

2 Visibility is not an end in itself, but a first step to success. High general attention can easily be gained by bizarre images (for example a gorilla in a jock strap), or by bare flesh, children, animals, famous faces. The important point is *relevance*, to the product and to its potential buyers and users.

3 Every advertisement must be clearly *branded*. If your brand name was replaced by another, would the advertisement work just as well? If your advertisement is not working hard it is wasting your money and at worst it may be working for your competitor.

4 An advertisement works harder when part of a coherent long-term campaign aimed at reinforcing the values of the brand. *Consistency* will pay off much better than one-off brilliance.

5 Customers do not buy products, they buy benefits. They will give their best attention to an advertisement which offers an answer to the question 'what's in it for me?'. Every successful advertisement *promises a benefit*.

them, and quite a few of them with literal minds never look for double meanings.

3 Creativity delivers memorability. Research into memory shows that an image is more easily recalled if it has one of the following properties: exaggeration, humour, absurdity, sensual appeal, colour, great simplicity, movement.

4 If no unique benefit exists for a brand, the campaign should try to pre-empt the high ground for the product category. Find out the key benefit for your market and promise it more clearly, more memorably and more effectively than your competition.

5 Testimonials work well if they come from experts in reputable companies. Athletes, comedians and other irrelevant celebrities simultaneously steal attention from the product and lose its credibility ('I bet he never drove a fork-lift truck in his life').

6 Demonstrations always score above average in recall or communication studies. It pays to visualise your promise. It saves time. It drives the message home. It is memorable.

7 Problem/solution is another above-average technique. You set up a problem the target reader can relate to and prove your product can solve it.

8 Never cheat with demonstrations or problem/solution ads. Your market is not stupid, and the world is full of whistle blowers, including your competitors.

9 If your product is new, tell people. Your market is always on the look-out for new improved products and new ways to use old products.

10 Headlines get five times the readership of body copy. Your headlines must offer something to the reader.

11 'Flagging the sufferer' is an excellent device. As David Ogilvy pointed out, the word 'rheumatism' in a headline will attract the attention of every reader with pain in the joints while encouraging the rest to pass on. Where a product is purchased by a readily identifiable market segment, it pays to flag them in the headline: 'problems with your computers?', 'fleet-owners!', 'over 30 and no company pension scheme?' and so on.

12 Long or short copy? Readership falls off rapidly after 50 words, but drops little more between 50 and 500 words. If your promise needs long copy, do not be afraid to use it.

13 Body copy is seldom read by more than 10 per cent of readers of trade and technical publications. But that 10 per cent means *your prospects*, and what you say to them determines your response rate. Body copy should use short sentences (around 12 words), short paragraphs (not more than three sentences), and use Anglo-Saxon words rather than Latin terminology.

14 Photographs tend to work harder than line illustrations. They are more believable, more memorable (and pull more coupons).

15 Story appeal can be built into pictures. The best results are achieved by photographs which suggest a story. The reader says to himself 'what goes on here?' and reads the copy to find out.

16 Captions should appear under all photographs. They get twice the readership of the body copy. Each caption should make an important copy point.

17 There is no such thing as a boring product, only boring advertising. Products and their benefits are always interesting to someone thinking of putting up the money to buy one. Advertising that tries to trick the unconcerned reader into being interested misses the point and is destined to fail.

18 In advertisement layout, less is more. Every advertisement needs a focal point and one big picture works better than several small ones.

19 The role of typography is to make an advertisement logical and easy to read. Copy gets lower readership if it is reversed out (printed white on black) or over-printed on illustrations.

20 Outstanding creative work is not for the faint-hearted. If a campaign is genuinely original, it is by definition untried. 'Creative' advertising requires the commitment of agency and client. If your market need is to play for safety, put the fact in the brief, and money in the budget for pre-testing everything.

TV OR NOT TV?

A point of controversy in business marketing is the use of television. The general public (and its political leaders) tend to equate all the effects of advertising, both good and bad, to television commercials. In studies of recall, consumers typically claim that any advertising they have seen for a brand was on television, irrespective of whether the advertiser had or had not used that medium. Multiple retailers are reluctant to stock goods which are not advertised on TV. Advertising professionals acknowledge TV to be the most impressive and intrusive medium, but also the most expensive per impact.

As a result, in Europe and North America, most leading brands of fast-moving consumer goods are advertised on television, often exclusively so. But the great majority of business-to-business advertising is placed in print, in specialised business newspapers and a wide range of professional, trade and technical magazines.

Should business advertisers ever use television? If so, under what circumstances, and how can it be used most effectively? To what extent can experience of consumer advertising be carried over?

In practice, some business advertisers, particularly those with large budgets, do use television. They do so for a number of reasons. One is not a good one: because they use a consumer advertising agency, who tend to recommend what they know well and are best at doing.

There are four far better motives:

(i)   to generate immediate visibility and reputation for the activities of a large, but relatively unknown company
(ii) to impress all parts of customer DMUs, particularly top management, and also the financial community
(iii) to build quickly awareness of a new product introduction
(iv) to gain a marketing edge over lower spending, or to match higher spending competitors.

Opting to use television or not is a question of weighing up objectively the key characteristics of TV as a medium.

For:

- *High impact.* Television is the most powerful and intrusive medium, given an adequate level of spend.
- *TV is the most 'public' medium.* Customers, distributors, sales-force and staff, together with their friends and contacts, will see the campaign.

Against:

- *TV is crudely targeted.* Even if carefully bought, it can be highly wasteful in its coverage compared with other specialised media.
- *It is expensive*, both in terms of the media cost per spot and the production cost of the commercial.

In practice, the reasons for setting aside these large objections in the context of a business-to-business audience usually rest on the potential effects expected from a specific campaign. If used under the right conditions, television has sometimes achieved its creative objective not only more effectively than print, but also more cost-effectively.

TELEVISION AS A CREATIVE MEDIUM

Experience in business markets has identified some guiding principles specific to TV advertising.

Television gives high impact, but the viewer's attention cannot be taken for granted, it has to be won. A commercial break is a cluttered medium, which competes not only with sampling other channels ('zapping') but also human needs (visits to the kitchen or the loo, conversation or reading). To overcome this, a successful commercial must grab attention at its opening and then rapidly involve its specific target audience. The stereotyped, banal cliché will not do this; it is better to show viewers something they have never seen before. Even then, it is safest to book the first slot in a break: the audience may have got away before you get the chance to grab them!

All successful commercials are built round a simple, strong idea which makes a promise relevant to their target audience. Usually there is a key frame in the commercial that captures this idea.

As said earlier, powerful images, humorous situations, famous personalities and references to well-known films can all gain attention – but this is too often at the expense of the product and the promise. Too many viewers remember the commercial but forget the brand. Each one must be clearly branded.

Research shows that if people like your advertising, they are more likely to buy your product. So 'entertainment' can be highly effective, but only if it too is clearly branded and contains a relevant promise.

Agency creative departments like television, because it offers the creative opportunities of sound, movement and colour. But these should be used with care. Research consistently says that the same message should hit the eye and ear at the same time. For example, a voice-over should comment on what the viewer can actually see.

Television is an excellent medium for product demonstrations, which always score highly for their ability to persuade. They do not have to be dull, some of the most entertaining TV commercials have been based on 'torture tests' where a demonstration has been taken to extremes.

By contrast, television is not good for complicated messages. Products with a long message need long copy, and that means press.

Long-term consistency is vital in any advertising. Inconsistency of message or tone of voice will inevitably lead to a blurred positioning – and this is particularly true of TV.

On the other hand, everything is possible with TV, the technicians these days can produce anything you ask for. The only limit is your imagination!

HOW TO GET THE BEST CREATIVE WORK FROM YOUR AGENCY

This is a true story. A Creative Director was once sitting in his office with a slightly unhappy client. During their chat, the client took an advertisement from his briefcase and placed it on the table. 'Why?' he asked, 'cannot I have advertising like that?'

The Creative Director found it hard not to smile: it was one of his own department's advertisements. Moreover, the Writer, Art Director and Account Handler responsible for this campaign were the ones who worked on the client's account; the product was somewhat less exciting, and the campaign budget was actually smaller.

He – the client – was the difference.

In fact, behind every great campaign is an advertiser who understands not only how to brief and evaluate work, but also how to create an atmosphere in which great work can happen. Here follow 20 factors that experience shows are important to clients who seek to get the very best work from their agency.

1: Ask for great advertising

Do not be embarrassed to use the word great. You will never get great work unless you have an appetite for greatness. This is where it must begin: with you, the client. To quote David Ogilvy again, 'A client gets the advertising he deserves.' Those who want great advertising, ask for it. Better still, they demand it and accept the consequences.

2: Radiate confidence in your agency

Confidence breeds enthusiasm and it takes enthusiastic people to produce great creative work.

3: Make sure your agency believes in your product

Introduce the agency people to the enthusiasts within your own company: designers, product managers and salespeople. Organise agency visits to some satisfied customers. It is amazing what your agency can do when they truly believe in a product. Conversely, they find it difficult to create great advertising for a product if their heart is not really in it, or if they do not understand what it is for or why anybody would want one. Look how much better advertising for computers has become since creative departments have been given them and learned how to exploit them!

4: Act as though creativity is important

Small gestures can make big impressions. For example, if the copywriter is in your meeting, refer to his work as 'the copy' (not the blurb, or rhubarb, or the grey lines). Make a point of reading it all and if you like it, tell him. From that point, he will be prepared to walk on blazing coals for you.

5: Brief problems not solutions

There is a great temptation to ask for a specific type of execution: a testimonial, a product demonstration, an editorial style approach. It sounds reasonable but it leads to mediocrity. It is better to concentrate on defining the precise problem that advertising must solve. If you can find 'originality' in the problem, it helps the agency to devise an original solution.

6: Do not be stingy with praise

Creative people take a good many knocks. They get used to it, in the way that professional footballers get used to bruises. But it hurts all the same. So, when you think an idea is elegant, ingenious or witty, say so. Or fax an instant response to the creative team. Applause is manna to creative people.

7: *Give your agency the right to be wrong*

Great advertising is brave and provocative. When it misses the mark, it is often by a mile! You should encourage your agency to take risks, and bring you their most ambitious ideas. As soon as creative people start to censor their own ideas, your chances of getting great advertising fall dramatically. Encourage an atmosphere where ideas can be rejected, but people never feel they are.

8: *Be consistent*

Creative people look to you for a clear set of logical principles. This helps them to fix the tone of voice of the advertising. (For example, when it comes to the use of humour.)

9: *Keep the approval process simple*

The ideal creative climate is one brilliant client working with one brilliant creative team. Obviously, this is not practical in big companies. But the nearer you can come to it, the better the results. At all costs, avoid decision making by committee. Committee meetings can end in a compromise and still be successful. Advertising ideas cannot.

10: *Insist on one creative recommendation*

A cynical agency will produce a raft of bad ideas in the hope that a half-good one will look brilliant. You should demand that your agency gives you a recommendation. This forces them to nail their colours to the mast. After all, this is what you are paying them for: to give you what is, in their judgement, the best possible solution. They should believe one of their ideas to be better than the others (should they not?), and in that case why would they ever show you (or you want to see) their second-best?

11: Master the fine art of evaluating work

Always deal with important issues first: the quality of the idea and the relevance of the proposition. (It is disheartening for an agency to spend half an hour discussing body copy and discover that the strategy has shifted.)

12: Be honest with your agency

Tell them everything about the product, including its weaknesses. Do not assume that by flying blind, the agency will avoid any tricky issues. It is just as likely that they will produce creative work which cannot run because of the unstated problem.

13: Do not try to salvage ideas

Headlines and visuals should be an integrated whole. It is difficult to keep one and change the other without weakening the idea. Your creative team would much sooner start again, with a revised brief, and so should you. (A reworked idea is a bit like reheated food. It is not much fun to prepare and usually is not very exciting to receive.)

14: Ask your agency how you can be a better client

The members of a creative department were asked to evaluate various clients. One was voted 'most preferred' by as many as 41 per cent of the department. The most common reasons given were 'creative freedom' and 'receptivity to new ideas'. Thirty-nine per cent voted a different client the one they would least like to work for. The most common reasons given were: 'too little creative freedom', 'too many levels of decision to go through' and 'more emphasis placed on research than on creative thinking'. All accounts are not created equal. And creative people do their best work on the accounts on which they prefer to work.

15: Avoid the 'big' presentation

It puts your agency in a position where they feel obliged to 'sell'. Review advertising in an informal atmosphere of partnership. It makes for a more constructive meeting.

16: Talk to your customers

Please do not pass on to the agency what your juniors tell you they think about the advertising. Instead, spend a day out with the salesforce. Ask your customers why they buy your products. Maybe take someone from the agency along while you do it. The better they know your customers, the more fruitful the dialogue their advertising will have with them.

17: Make sure the agency feels responsible for creating the campaign

Be a leader, not a nitpicker. Tell the agency what is wrong, and why, not how to fix it.

18: Insist that the head of your company takes a personal interest in the advertising

Nothing is more discouraging to agency people than to have creative work rejected by someone they meet only once a year, or worse still, never.

19: Share advertising results with the agency, both good and bad

Certainly, coupon returns and campaign awareness results are essential but so are letters and customer comments. This type of response is less scientific but it can sometimes be more illuminating.

20: Give your agency time to do the job

After all, you would not put a new product on the market overnight. Neither should they.

And there you have it. Twenty clues to make your advertising work better than the competitors', and twenty ways to provide the kind of input, create the atmosphere, and apply the judgements that can help you get such creative work from your agency.

9

MEDIA: HITTING THE TARGET COST-EFFECTIVELY

*An effective media plan is one that maximises the number of potential
exposures to the selected target audience within the pre-determined
budget*

INTRODUCTION

In *How to Succeed in Business-to-business Advertising* (Primary
Contact and Reed Business Publishing, 1988) it was stated:

> An advertising budget is wasted, even if the media provides a rele-
> vant and willing reader, if the attention is not caught or if nothing of
> interest or importance is communicated.

To achieve success, it is obvious that the creative approach and
the media must work together. This will ensure that both strategic and tactical objectives are met; and that joint decisions are
made on tactical implementation (size, colour, frequency, positioning, choice of vehicle).

PLANNING

Of the two major functions within the media department, *Planning* and *Buying*, the most critical is planning. If the plan is not
appropriate, even outstanding creative work will be wasted.
Every aspect of planning must be geared to achieving maximum

exposure of the creative message to the selected target audience. To achieve this, the major steps are:

- setting the objectives
- selecting the correct target audience
- the inter-media decision (should we select TV, press or another medium?)
- the intra-media decision (if press, what publications?).

The most fundamental factor which will affect the final media direction is a specific and clear-cut objective. It is vital that the media function is involved at the *earliest* possible stage in the overall planning cycle, as it is likely to have the most significant contribution to make to the overall campaign shape. Creative needs are important and should also be discussed early (for example, desirability of colour, movement, long copy, unusual shapes and sizes). However, the main input should come from the media planner, based usually on target audience, size and budget and cost-efficiency.

SETTING THE OBJECTIVES

Each individual medium (posters, cinema, TV, and so on) has its own specific characteristics. For example, certain types of media are very good for generating direct response, while others are strong at creating awareness.

It is therefore essential that at the outset of any plan detailed media objectives are set arising from the advertising objectives, which in turn derive from the marketing objective. Wherever possible, these objectives should be quantified (for example, to achieve cover in excess of 75 per cent of our audience, with an average of two 'opportunities-to-see' per buying cycle). It is against these objectives, agreed with the client, that the final success of the media plan should be judged.

SELECTING THE CORRECT TARGET AUDIENCE

Anyone who has been involved with business-to-business marketing will know that this is one of the most difficult areas. In consumer advertising the task is more straightforward as usually there is a single relevant person acting as specifier and purchaser thus making targeting simple (for example, housewives aged 25-44 in ABC1 socio-economic group).

In business markets the situation is far more complex. In the first place (as discussed in Chapter 2) there are typically eight stages in a major buying decision, each subject to five basic types of influence:

(i)   the authoriser
(ii)   the specifier
(iii) the specialist adviser
(iv)   the purchaser
(v)   the final user.

Within each of these categories of influence there could be involved a number of people, at all levels in the company and who perform a multiplicity of relevant functions.

It therefore becomes critical that no relevant individual is overlooked at this stage. And it is important to get the balance right between functions by applying weighting factors against which the media profiles should be matched. This task is usually carried out with a combination of agency experience, client knowledge and whenever possible quantified market intelligence. Once the objectives and target audience have been set, the overall strategic direction must be considered and the first part of this exercise is to select the main media type.

THE INTER-MEDIA DECISION

This is the process by which the major media type is selected. In the business-to-business field the choice of candidate media is very broad, including not only conventional 'above-the-line' media (TV, press, etc) but also those known historically as 'below-the-line' (direct mail, PR, exhibitions and so on). This was discussed further in Chapter 7.

Although statistical data will be of paramount importance, subjective factors also come into play. It is here that there must be a close liaison between media and creative.

On the statistical side, the obvious areas to look at will be capital cost, profile, coverage of target audience and cost-effectiveness; but equally important will be each medium's likely ability to meet the specific objectives through factors such as its ability to create impact, build awareness, reinforce image, stimulate response and so on.

Last but not least are the creative considerations: are colour, movement, sound, etc, essential, desirable or unnecessary?

There will never be standardised reasons for choosing a given medium, nor need there be. Each new campaign needs to be judged in its own right, *always* (and only) against the set objectives.

THE INTRA-MEDIA DECISION

Having selected the main media type, it is then necessary to decide how best to use it. Here one is looking at details such as the editorial authority of one publication versus another, or the programme context for TV and radio, the location of posters and so on.

If *general business* or *consumer* media are being used, the task is made simpler by the availability of good, well-accepted syndicated research sources: JICNARS, TGI, BARB, BMRC. With the aid of computer analysis the most cost-effective combination of publications, national newspapers and TV stations can be arrived at.

If *trade and technical* media are being used, the situation is more complex. With few exceptions, good research data will not exist – apart from raw data on circulation and circulation profile. The most important factor of all, however, will be experience, and more subjective issues (such as editorial environment) come into play.

The combined experience of client and agency is of great value. Past response data, and factors such as sales-force feedback should be taken into account. The task of a planner in the business arena is not an easy one. He or she will invariably be faced with an over-crowded magazine marketplace, with up to 80 journals covering a given audience and without reliable, independent comparative research. Hence the importance of experience.

BUYING

Good buying can make or break a campaign. Once the plan is correctly developed it is essential the media are bought at the most cost-effective rate. Heavy emphasis must be applied to making every client's pound work as hard as possible. There is absolutely no point in negotiating a very cheap rate if the advertisement does not receive maximum exposure. Relevant positioning of the advertisement within magazines and newspapers can sometimes be crucial – and as much emphasis should be placed on this as on securing the right rate.

As there are many subjective issues involved, both at the planning and buying level in the business field, one of the most important assets of a planner/buyer is his or her knowledge of individual publishing companies. To ensure best possible results, in-depth relationships must be built, not only with the immediate contacts but with the management and marketing teams of the key media companies.

VOUCHERING

Although an administrative function, its importance should not be understated. Vouchers are the official evidence to a client that the advertisement has appeared as ordered. They also act as a quality control check to the agency on positioning and reproduction quality.

SUMMARY

In one sentence, the role of a successful media department is: to place an advertisement in the right environment in the right medium, at the right time, at the right price, in order to convert an opportunity-to-see into an **impact**: a real exposure of the advertising message to its target.

10

THE IMPORTANCE OF
BRANDING

How to turn a commodity into a premium-priced capital asset

INTRODUCTION

Many experienced marketers take the importance of branding for granted. However, the senior management of more than a few industrial organisations have achieved their success through excellence in disciplines other than marketing. And they, while instinctively feeling that branding must be important, need to understand more clearly why this is so.

'Why,' they say, 'should I spend money on branding? What will I get in return?' This chapter sets out to answer these questions in the light of experience.

DEFINITION OF BRANDING

Branding is the active and consistent projection of the qualities which differentiate an organisation, its product or service from its competition.

A *strongly branded* market is one where the customers hold the competitive brands to be significantly different and take these differences into account when making choices. A market with weak branding or none at all is known as a *commodity market*.

THE NATURE OF A BRAND

A brand can differentiate itself by one or a number of factors, intended to appeal to the buyer, user or investor (and anyone who influences their decision) in the form of 'added values'. These can be tangible, intangible or a combination, for example:

- **product specification:** more, better or preferred ingredients; a wider range of sizes, colourways, concentrations, purities; thicker protective coatings; recycled raw materials or higher-quality components; improved or longer-lasting performance; ease of assembly or application; indeed any 'product plus' recognisable by and helpful to the purchaser.

- **service:** guarantees such as 'or your money back'; on-site inspection, installation, training or repairs; up-dates or enhancements included free; round-the-clock ordering and helplines; JIT delivery; subsidised technical advice and after-sales service; anything which the buyer can interpret as 'if anything goes wrong they will see me right'.

- **reputation and image:** sound business practice and probity; approachability; reliability, guarantees; user prestige; technological break-throughs; environmental awareness; 'traditional values'; anything whereby the buyer will feel reassured that the choice has been the right one.

As the reputation of a brand becomes stronger among the community of buyers and users, its supplier will be able progressively to reduce his dependence on price in marketing. Weak brands are usually forced to use price as a major selling tool, whereas a strong brand may even be able to compete successfully almost irrespective of price. Creating a strong brand name and image is an expensive process and not instant. Yet, once established, it can be economical to maintain.

There are examples from consumer marketing (where the strategy has been understood for a long time) of strong brands retaining market leadership for over a century. Accountancy has in consequence recognised that a brand property is a capital asset, similar to 'goodwill', and that its ownership should be valued in the balance sheet. For example, Nestlé bought Rowntree Mackintosh and Ford bought Jaguar at a multiple of the value of their physical assets.

Good current examples of strong brands in the business-to-business field include:

- American Express
- ICI
- JCB
- Rolls Royce
- Shell.

The ultimate success is when the brand name becomes the generic term for the whole market (such as Polaroid or Xerox). All competitors are to some extent thereby down-graded to 'me-toos', and a distributor who supplies them against a generic order risks prosecution for 'passing off'!

THE BENEFITS OF A STRONG BRAND

Economically speaking, branding reduces the price-elasticity of the product compared with its immediate competition. This enables the supplier to obtain a higher volume or a higher market share at the same price, or alternatively a premium price for the same volume (see Chapter 3).

Besides price and volume, the benefits of a strong brand can manifest themselves in a number of ways:

(i)   high customer loyalty and more regular repeat purchasing
(ii)   easier sales negotiations with less acrimonious customer complaints
(iii) premium prices and easier price increases
(iv)   easier cross-selling of other products in range and making new introductions
(v)   differences can be protected so that competitors will have difficulty in matching without appearing 'me-toos'
(vi)   greater resistance to competitive promotions and launches.

THE BENIGN AND VICIOUS SPIRALS

By contrast, in commodity markets where there is only weak branding or none at all, customers differentiate between suppliers only on price. In such circumstances, customers tend to concentrate their purchases on the lowest-price suppliers. Price-elasticity is high, or soon becomes so.

This puts heavy pressure on suppliers to cut prices if they wish to build or even maintain volume. As a result profit margins are squeezed, and suppliers are forced to cut costs to stay in business.

They do this where they can: typically first by decimating marketing effort (usually by firing sales staff and cutting advertising), then by eliminating customer services (such as free helplines, extended credit or delivery on demand) and even as a last resort by reducing product specification. All this makes the product harder to sell, requiring yet deeper price cuts. This forms a vicious spiral, leading eventually to the departure of all but the very largest or lowest-cost suppliers.

Alternatively, where a manufacturer can differentiate a product by branding, its prices can be raised. This will lose volume, but at lower price-elasticities both revenue and margins will improve. Diverting part of this revenue to product improvement and then promoting it, will re-build customer acceptance and regain the lost volume. This is a benign spiral which can then be repeated, yet further differentiating the brand above the commodity suppliers, and increasing customer loyalty.

ESTABLISHING AND COMMUNICATING THE BRAND

To be a true brand, it has to be widely known and recognised easily by the purchaser at the point of sale and ideally throughout its working life. This may be achieved in a number of ways, as appropriate:

- Appearance
- Packaging (design and method)
- Image
- Selling method
- Customer support
- Literature.

Purchasers, potential purchasers and their advisers (and even those who reject it) should be aware and regularly reminded of the distinctive features of the brand. Every part of the marketing mix should be integrated to reinforce this: selling activity, price policy, distribution, advertising, direct mail, sponsorship, trade fairs, customer seminars, public relations and so on.

Discrepancies (such as inadequate packaging, unreliable deliveries, poor technical support, weak or inappropriate advertising) can undermine a high-quality brand image.

Fig. 10.1 The benign and vicious circles

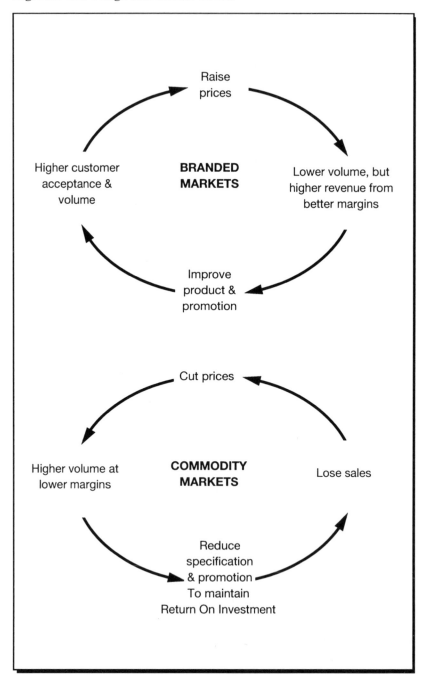

Advertising is the traditional spearhead of a strong brand image and one of the cheapest ways of reinforcing it, but cannot act as a substitute for product quality or good customer service.

SUMMARY

Branding is a marketing technique which differentiates a good or a service (or its supplier) from its competition. It should be undertaken for specific and quantifiable purposes both short- and long-term:

a short-term purposes

- to establish an advantage over competition
- to provide a focus for marketing
- to gain preference during the buying cycle
- to reassure existing customers
- to attract new customers.

b long-term purposes

- to build stable and positive perceptions
- to gain lasting advantages in price, volume and market share
- to provide a defence against competitive attack
- to provide a base for the launch of new developments
- to encourage a sense of achievement amongst existing and potential staff.

Without branding, a product becomes a 'commodity', thereby risking a number of serious penalties:

- customers believe they can switch suppliers without loss

- customers tend to choose 'the cheapest', with little or no loyalty
- marketing effort has to concentrate on price instead of quality of product and back-up services
- profits are squeezed, demanding cuts in marketing effort and product quality, which make sales even more difficult to get.

Establishing a strong brand is not an overnight process, and requires integration of all parts of the company's operations towards adding values and communicating them to customers. If successful, branding will improve the 'bottom line' of the brand in the short term, and the valuation of the whole company in the long term.

11

HOW RESEARCH CAN HELP IN THE CREATION OF EFFECTIVE ADVERTISING

What can we do to improve our chances of success?

THE FOUR STAGES OF ADVERTISING RESEARCH

While it is widely agreed that good advertising works, nobody has yet developed any generally accepted explanation of *how* it works, despite two generations of market research on the subject. This means that advertising (in common with all other business activities) can offer no guarantees of success. Nevertheless, research can perform the same functions here as it does elsewhere: namely, minimise the risks of serious failure, provide clues for developing potential improvements, and give objective support to sound creative judgement.

Aside from *media* research which is usually dealt with at industry level, and a subject somewhat too esoteric for this book, leading advertisers and their agencies commonly research their customers to assist in the development of effective advertising, at four distinct stages:

(i) Strategic
(ii) Developmental
(iii) Evaluative
(iv) Assessment.

For any campaign which will need large sums of money spent over several years, all four stages should be considered essential, and can be expected to justify their cost. Yet low-budget or short-run advertising can also benefit from the *selective* use of research. This concept is commonplace in fast-moving packaged goods. This chapter attempts to demonstrate that the principles and techniques originally developed elsewhere can be adapted to the needs of business-to-business advertising.

Fig. 11.1 Four stages of advertising research

1 **Strategic** – to set objectives

2 **Developmental** – to help direct creative work along the most promising lines

3 **Evaluative** – to reassure the advertiser the recommended campaign is on target

4 **Campaign assessment** – to track trends in the market, to identify the effects on target customers of advertising and other marketing activity by us and by competition

In particular:

- purchasing and usage behaviour

- attitudes to the product category

- images of the leading brands.

THE NEED FOR EARLY RESEARCH

If it is to make a useful contribution, research must be built into the campaign plan from the very beginning. Research carried out at a late stage, often to resolve a dispute, rarely gives useful information, and often creates animosity between creatives, account management and clients.

Assessment research, which is inevitably carried out after the budget has been spent, can help only in planning *future* advertising. It should be done as part of the regular tracking of all marketing activity.

The Evaluation stage is done when finished material is available, inevitably close to deadline, so that only minor (and expensive) adjustments can be made as a result. Such research is usually done by the advertiser, to provide reassurance that the money will be wisely spent; and, more importantly, to help guide future strategy.

The top priority for advertising research money must be the Strategic and Developmental stages, and the earlier they are done the more cost-effective they will be. The rest of this chapter summarises some first-hand experience of how these types of research work best in business-to-business advertising.

THE IMPORTANCE OF BRIEFING

As discussed in Chapter 13, the fundamental of all successful advertising is a *market-based objective*. Many (if not most) campaign failures can be traced to failure at the briefing stage. *Strategic research* (into the market, products, prices, distributors, customers, competitors and past marketing activity) is therefore needed to determine the marketing objectives, particularly:

- market positioning
- target customers
- customer needs to be satisfied
- competitive benefits to be stressed.

All marketing activity should be co-ordinated to the same marketing objectives; and the distinct role for advertising in achieving them has to be specified at the briefing stage, as must the roles for every other technique to be used.

It is sensible (and also tactful) for the advertiser to discuss the objectives with the agency *before* they are finalised. The agency may well have useful ideas about strategy and the kind of research needed, and because they have been consulted the account team will understand their task better and be more enthusiastic about doing it well. Nevertheless, the setting of objectives and the strategic research on which they should be based is ultimately the responsibility of the advertiser. Chapter 13 discusses this issue in detail.

DEVELOPMENTAL RESEARCH

Developmental research means any pre-testing done to help the agency creative department to produce advertising which will achieve its agreed objectives. This is the responsibility of the agency to design, carry out and interpret. The research itself may be carried out either by the agency's own research staff, or by external specialists. Like everything done by an agency, it will be paid for by the client: whether as part of any general commission or fee arrangements, or as a separate item, depends on the terms of their contract.

A wise advertiser will give the agency wide scope to conduct developmental research how and when they feel they need it. Anything which improves the effectiveness of advertising (or avoids failure) will pay for itself many times over. Agencies which abuse or bias research to support bad recommendations, or 'sell' ideas not on the brief, quickly get found out and lose their clients. Good developmental research forms a 'hot-line' between creatives and target customers. Anything which improves the former's understanding of the latter must be of immediate benefit to the advertiser.

On the other hand, it is possible to do too much research. It is inevitably expensive and time-consuming, and some issues are of more importance than others. If 'everything' has to be researched, the discipline can stultify creativity ('don't bother, it will never get through the research!'). Advertising research, like all other types of research, should be concentrated where the risks are highest and the sums of money at stake are largest.

BASIC RULES FOR CREATIVE DEVELOPMENTAL RESEARCH

1 All should be aware that it is not possible to develop both a strategy and an execution from the same research project. *Agree the strategy* (after research if necessary) before moving on to the development stage.

2 *Test early, quickly and cheaply*, using rough materials and while ideas are still 'plastic' in the minds of the creatives.

3 *Test only against the agreed objectives*: all other criteria must be taken as irrelevant. Anything which it is important for the advertising to contain or do must be put into the brief (see Chapter 13). Similarly, *test only on the stated target audience*: it should not matter what anyone else thinks!

4 *Show alternative versions or treatments* wherever possible: people have trouble in reacting to a single stimulus, but can readily make comparisons and explain their reasons.

5 *Do not mix rough and finished advertisements*: your customers are not advertising experts and may respond more to a beautiful photograph than to the idea behind it. If you need to compare last year's campaign, turn it back to the same state of finish as this year's new developments.

6 *Never mix your advertisements with those of competitors*: it is unwise to assume they have the same advertising objectives as you, and the research readings may mislead you. It is perfectly possible for a competitor's campaign to be doing an excellent job for its sponsor, but have no effects at all against your own objectives. Further, it is best practice not to show for pre-test purposes advertisements which have already appeared. Some customers in the research will have seen some of them before (but not necessarily all), which makes it impossible to separate their reactions to the advertisements from their preconceptions about the different suppliers.

7 *Use qualitative methods*. Creatives prefer ideas to numbers, and at this stage need *diagnostics* – what worked or went wrong, and why? This kind of research will not show what is 'best' in an absolute sense, but will point up negatives, and indicate which approaches do and do not communicate what is intended.

8 Get the customers to *talk about the brand*, rather than act as conscious critics of advertisements. The reaction you are looking for is 'What a good product for my business', not 'What a clever/witty/exciting/eye-catching advertisement'.

9 *Use a researcher with relevant experience*, who understands and communicates with creatives, and is trusted by them. Developmental research must be seen as a help, not just another hurdle to be jumped (like the Creative Review Board and the Client meeting)!

Fig. 11.2 Rules for effective advertising research

1 Agree the strategy and objectives before starting to test.

2 Test early and quickly on rough material.

3 Test only on the target audience and against the agreed objectives.

4 Show alternative treatments of one product, not several competitors.

5 Use qualitative methods to give diagnostics about what was communicated: 'What kind of product is this?'

6 Use researchers who understand the problems and can give advice rather than pass judgement.

THE QUALITATIVE RESEARCH TECHNIQUE

Qualitative research is designed to collect information in depth from small numbers of people, and is in contrast with 'quantitative research' which surveys numbers large enough for statistical validity but inevitably covers a narrower field through predetermined questionnaires.

Qualitative research has long been commonplace in consumer markets, but has proved equally practicable and helpful in business-to-business. Its key techniques are the individual, extended, 'depth' interview, and the group discussion (known as a Focus Group in the USA). Both are conducted by specially-trained interviewers or 'moderators', who use short 'topic guides' instead of questionnaires to encourage respondents to express their views at length and in their own language or technical jargon. Groups of 6–10 people are particularly helpful because they will stimulate each other with only minimum guidance from the moderator.

Such discussions typically last one to $1\frac{1}{2}$ hours and are tape or video recorded. Stimulus material can readily be introduced, including competitive products, new product ideas briefly described or illustrated on 'concept boards' and alternative advertising treatments in rough form.

Analysis has to be more subjective and complex than in quantitative research. It requires an analyst (preferably not the moderator) to listen to the tapes to identify key areas and extract seminal quotations about them. This material is used by the moderator for discussion (debrief) with the survey sponsor and to form the basis of a full written report.

EVALUATIVE AND ASSESSMENT RESEARCH

To be of use, evaluation before exposure in the media of finished material has to be quantitative, and to focus on the limited topics believed (preferably as a result of the qualitative stages) to be most crucial. No technique for doing this has universal acceptance, and so in practice little research is carried out on campaigns which have been finalised but not yet launched.

Assessment of advertising campaigns after exposure is a complex matter because the effects of advertising have to be separated from those of other parts of the advertiser's marketing mix, competitive activity, and external market and economic factors. It forms the subject of Chapter 12.

SUMMARY

Research is now 'part of the furniture' of creating successful consumer advertising. Business-to-business has been slow to draw on the wealth of available experience.

However, there are no 'magic techniques' which work for all objectives, all products and all markets. It is better to do research early when it will have the most positive effect, and to budget the time and money to tailor-make the research to the problem.

Advertising research is part of the process of reducing risks. It is better at eliminating failures than spotting successes: really wild but good ideas sometimes get rejected with the rubbish. Consequently, over-researched advertising tends to be safe, dull and mainstream – although this may be what the market position of some brands demands.

Nevertheless, all advertising will be the better for properly researched objectives, and early pre-testing to refine ideas; success can even be improved upon in subsequent years if objectively assessed after the event.

12

HOW TO EVALUATE ADVERTISING CAMPAIGNS

How do we know it worked?

THE BASIC PHILOSOPHY: ADVERTISING IS ACCOUNTABLE

It is a central tenet of this book's philosophy that 'advertising is a cost unless it sells'. Yet advertising to business customers is too often seen as an 'act of faith': to be funded only when money is readily available, but cut back ruthlessly along with other 'expenses' in hard times.

Paradoxically, this results in concentrating advertising into periods when sales are easy to come by (and targets might be achieved without it), compared with times of sluggish customer demand or heavy competition when the salesforce needs all the help it can get.

The argument usually put forward to justify this behaviour is not that advertising is thought to be ineffective (no company would ever commission any if that were generally believed!), but that its proper evaluation is so difficult that it is better to concentrate funds where their results can be seen quickly and counted directly.

This book challenges this view because in recent years so much has been found out about the effects of advertising and how to measure them. While there is no simple 'magic technique' to cover all eventualities, it has been proved in practice that it is frequently possible to measure the effects of advertising, and to evaluate its cost-effectiveness in comparison with other ways of using the money (such as price cutting).

This is not a plea for bottomless budgets! Advertising can and should be as accountable as other business activities, and money should be spent on any of them only in so far as it can be demonstrated to pay for itself, at least in the long run.

THE PROBLEM OF MEASUREMENT

The problem lies in the demonstration itself. As pointed out in Chapter 5, Finance Directors understandably prefer to authorise money for activities whose effects can be seen directly (such as additional sales staff, extra price incentives and services to customers), or better still for tangible assets, which can be shown in the balance sheet and even sold off in emergency. For example, a fleet of new delivery vans can be costed in detail before purchase, and its performance subsequently logged, so that it can be evaluated as 'cost-effective' if costs-per-delivery are sufficiently below last year's.

Advertising suffers because its material is ephemeral, and its effects complex and varied. These may include creating awareness, reinforcing or changing attitudes, identifying new prospects, pre-selling a sales call, fighting off a take-over and generating actual sales off-the-page. Some of these happen immediately, others take time; some are readily checkable, others can be assessed only indirectly.

Further, advertising rarely acts in isolation (except perhaps in the case of a mail-order specialist whose sales come exclusively through advertisements). It is often difficult to take any particular sale and then isolate the contribution of advertising from that of the sales force, price, the performance of previous purchases, word-of-mouth, competitors' activity, economic trends and so on. Most of these have both long- and short-term effects, and may interact with each other.

Measuring advertising is therefore usually difficult and sometimes expensive, but (it can be postulated) rarely impossible: it can be achieved sufficiently often to justify making the attempt, and indeed persisting in the effort.

SPECIFIC AND RELEVANT OBJECTIVES ARE VITAL

The general tendency in the past has been to measure only such advertisement-related variables as 'awareness' or 'memorability', irrespective of whether raising these is desirable or even mentioned in the objectives. This is because they are relatively cheap and easy to measure, and indeed despite decades of evidence that there is no direct correlation between purchase of a brand and the memorability of its advertising. 'Magic number' techniques of this kind lead to very superficial and incomplete evaluation. Worse, agency creative departments are thereby distracted into 'beating the research norms' rather than selling the product.

The starting point for successful evaluation of a campaign is to agree in advance what effects the advertising should have in the marketplace. Often, objectives are set which are too general, for example: 'To sell more, of course!' Apart from the equally obvious point that no company ever spends money to *prevent* sales, advertising can also legitimately be used to help support prices, or minimise a decline in a bad year, or to build loyalty by reassuring buyers how well they have chosen after a sale has taken place.

A company will plan a level of sales income (which implies both a volume and a price), and expect a number of activities to contribute to this. The objective set for advertising within this plan should define its specific role in generating these sales. (This should ideally be unique because if two or more activities have exactly the same role, it is logical to transfer all the money to the one believed the most cost-effective.) Further, if effectiveness is later to be measured, the objectives will have to be expressed in *quantified* terms.

Therefore advertising (and every other activity in the marketing mix) needs to have its objectives set specifically: whom it is aimed at (by company, job title, influence on purchase, even by name), what advertising is intended to do for them, and what action it is hoped they will take as a result. Chapter 13 discusses the nature, content of and approach to a brief for an outside agency.

CLEAR ACTION STANDARDS LEAD TO GOOD DATA

Once these objectives have been specified, it is possible to set the vital quantified *action standards* for success: about the advertising itself, the effects it should have on the target audience and what effects these in turn should have on sales and profits.

Just as each advertising campaign is likely to have different objectives, so each may well need different evaluation systems. The action standards themselves will indicate what needs to be monitored.

For example, if we want 90 per cent of the market to know about our new product six months after launch, we must set in hand a survey of awareness among potential buyers. If we have asked for new sales leads, we must set up a system for logging enquiries, including those who telephone or call in person as well as those who return our coupons. If we intend to improve our market rating for quality compared with competition we must set in hand a series of attitude tracking studies, or subscribe to a syndicated corporate image study (if such exists).

Some of these measurements will be internal to the company, and may already have been collected for several past years. If so, this is excellent because past trends can be identified, and the effects of changes in advertising weight or strategy will show up more quickly. It is important to check that the information is fully and correctly recorded, and in a form that facilitates analysis.

On the other hand, interpretation will be complicated because data such as sales, profits, order-to-call ratios, enquiries, and customer complaints are affected not by advertising alone but by other marketing activities, and by interaction between them.

MARKET RESEARCH FOR EVALUATION

In addition to these internal monitors, other measurements will be needed which relate to the outside world, particularly customers' and distributors' attitudes and behaviour. To monitor changes here will almost inevitably demand market research, particularly interviews with valid samples of target buyers. It is usually advisable to commission outside professional help rather than use company staff. Salesforces, for example, have no technical training in surveys, ought to have a vested interest in obtaining favourable results, and should not have any spare time available during normal sales calls to administer evaluation questionnaires!

Mail or telephone surveys are sometimes appropriate, but both need the benefit of professional design and an independent cover name to obtain adequate response rates (an absolute minimum of 50 per cent is necessary to make the results worth scrutiny, 80 per cent is better and possible). Indeed any overt interaction between supplier and customers must inevitably lack objectivity because the customers will expect anything they say to be used in later sales negotiations and will bias their responses accordingly.

Collection of company internal data is likely to be cheap, but will include the effects of the whole marketing effort. External data will be more specific, but cost money to collect. While in many cases the sums required are quite small, professional market research among customers can sometimes be expensive. It is best in all cases to allocate adequate funds to do the job properly, as inaccurate or inappropriate data will mislead the company into incorrect and unprofitable decisions. If professional advice is considered too expensive, it is usually better to do without altogether than to compromise. Amateur market research can be as dangerous to a company as amateur brain surgery would be to an individual!

By definition, the results of research are not known in advance and cannot be guaranteed. Yet experience shows that few advertising campaigns cannot be improved continually, at least in detail and sometimes substantially, by the consistent feed-back of the results of market research.

Hence, research can be set 'action standards' of its own. Quite modest improvements in the effectiveness of the creative content of a campaign, or of the efficiency of its media-plan in hitting its target, will pay for sufficient evaluation research. For example, with an advertising budget of £200 000, it is theoretically justifiable to spend up to £20 000 of it on research which indicates grounds for 10 per cent improvement in the effectiveness of the rest. Judgement of the likelihood of being able to do this will improve with experience.

ASSESSMENT OF RESULTS

Having obtained reliable data, the main problems of interpretation will lie in separating the effects of advertising from those of the advertiser's other marketing activities and from uncontrollable market variables such as competitive activity or interest rates.

There are three approaches: first, by setting objectives and measurements (as suggested above) which are unique to advertising so that most other causes of change can be eliminated.

Second, by using multi-variate analysis techniques such as econometric modelling. These methods are complex and specialised but have shown a number of successes in identifying the cost-effectiveness or otherwise of advertising in consumer markets. They can be adapted to business-to-business situations provided there is an adequate database to analyse: namely time series of readings of sales and a variety of internal, market and general economic factors that might affect purchasing.

The third approach is experimental marketing. While a market is not a laboratory and many of the influences on buyers' behaviour are not controllable, it is often possible to vary one component of the marketing mix (such as advertising weight, media plan or content) between one area, customer industry or season and another. This will help to isolate its effects.

ADVERTISING IS AN INVESTMENT, NOT AN EXPENSE

Advertising (and any other marketing activity) can have its cost-effectiveness evaluated, providing the company concerned regards it as a serious business activity, rather than just a 'tactical luxury' to be tolerated in good years and ruthlessly cut whenever there are problems with the cash-flow.

Fig. 12.1 The evaluation process

Advertising can be made an accountable process by extending to it the same degree of consistency and objectivity that is used on other business decisions. The process to be followed is parallel to conventional 'management by objectives'.

The necessary sequence is:

1 Set specific and quantified objectives for advertising within the marketing plan, arising from the company's long-term corporate goals.

2 Set up monitoring systems to collect the relevant data.

3 Analyse the data obtained carefully and objectively to isolate the effects of advertising from other company and market influences on sales. Evaluate the impact of these effects on 'the bottom line'.

4 Undertake regular market experiments to 'beat the norms' and encourage continuous improvement in advertising effectiveness.

5 Evaluate only against pre-determined action standards.

Whether any set of results counts as success or failure can never be decided *after* the event: an agency tends to hail any positive change as a victory, their client always feels this much could have been achieved without advertising at all!

Experience shows that while advertising has immediate effects, it is nevertheless a strategic marketing technique, whereby most of its effects are long-term and cumulative. Successful advertising acts more like a capital investment, building up goodwill, and less like an expense.

This is why consistency in spend and content is so important, and why 'stop/go' is dangerous. While there are usually benefits in 'up-front weighting' to get a new campaign off the ground quickly, it is always better to set budgets at a reasonable level which can be maintained for several years in succession, in preference to spending a much larger sum in the launch year of a new campaign, if this risks leaving the product unsupported for a lengthy period while the money is being recouped from sales.

Once advertising is viewed as an investment, it then becomes necessary to identify the required long-term return on it. This will help to define the action standards for success in relation to profits, which in their turn will pinpoint the information needed to make the assessments.

THE LONG-TERM PAY-OFF

There is a pleasant surprise awaiting those who take the time and trouble to evaluate in this way. They will find that their advertising is (or can progressively be made) highly effective; and that, if so, it will almost always prove more cost-effective than many other highly regarded sales builders such as price cutting.

The research summarised in Chapters 3 and 4 has found that:

- goods and services which are seen as higher quality justify and get higher prices
- sales people who are well supported sell more – and discount less

● relatively small increases in volume and especially price often have a substantial effect on net profits.

Once set in hand, an evaluation system can be used to make constant improvements in cost-effectiveness, and so will justify its trouble and expense many times over.

13

BRIEFING THE AGENCY FOR SUCCESS

Most failures in advertising were built in at the briefing stage

HOW BRIEFING CAN CREATE FAILURE

Advertising agencies like to publicise their successes, but rarely discuss failure. Yet advertising, like any business decision, involves both art and science, and is a matter of balancing rewards and risks. While success can never be guaranteed in the real world, this book proposes that the causes at least of major failure can often be foreseen through research and experience and so avoided.

Experience (see Chapters 11 and 12) suggests that many (perhaps most) failures in advertising can be traced to the briefing stage. Such failures can be of one of six types:

(i)   no adequate brief (perhaps none at all) provided in the first place
(ii) the brief did not specify the full requirements of the client, or did not accurately reflect the situation in the marketplace
(iii) the brief was not properly communicated to, or understood by, the agency
(iv) the brief was changed later (for example, at the approval of creative strategy or even final assessment stage)
(v)   the agency did not implement the brief
(vi) the campaign was on brief but did not perform adequately.

The last category needs little discussion. It is not totally unknown for a pre-tested and approved execution of a good brief to fail, perhaps (in an imperfect world) because of an unexpected move by a competitor, or of inadequate creativity. Yet a Type (vi) failure is rare, and then often unavoidable. More hopefully, the problem in such cases is usually one of degree: insufficient success rather than total disaster.

THE BESETTING SINS OF ADVERTISING

Types (iv) and (v) illustrate basic breaches in agency–client relations. One of the easiest ways for a client to demoralise an otherwise effective agency is to turn down a proposed campaign (especially at a late stage in its development) for reasons unconnected with the brief ('we need coupon response', 'we thought you would want to major on our sense of ecological responsibility', 'our Chairman is averse to cartoons'). This syndrome, *moving the goalposts in the course of the game*, can quickly reduce the best of creatives to gibbering impotence!

The corresponding iniquity on the part of agencies is *backing into the strategy*. The agency attempts to sell a creative approach which is brilliant and highly original but with no apparent relation to the product or its users, by advocating: 'we realise this is not quite on brief, but for such a wonderful idea, couldn't we reconsider . . .?' It can be argued that the besetting sin of the whole advertising business is irrelevance, and ignoring an agreed brief is one sure way to engender it.

Such behaviour comes from not understanding the nature of a brief or from devaluing its importance. A brief is an *action plan* which specifies how some activity is expected to contribute to achieving central objectives, and through which different activities are co-ordinated.

BRIEFING IS THE ADVERTISER'S TASK

Agencies surprisingly often find that their brief consists of a statement of budget with a few informal pointers to the direction in which the current campaign might develop. Without a more specific brief, the agency has the freedom to suggest whatever it thinks best, but will be aware that the client has an equal right to turn down their proposals for any reason whatever. So, before incurring any costs, a professional agency will start by writing its own detailed brief, and then ask the client to approve it for their mutual protection.

But no advertiser should let any supplier produce their own brief. Advertising does not take place in isolation, and must be integrated with a variety of other activities, many of which (at least in a business-to-business context) will have larger budgets, and be carried out by the client's own staff. While it is sometimes appropriate to have the marketing plan advertising-led, the client cannot expect the agency to have a fully detailed view of the total implications of his business plan, and so should not delegate to the agency the responsibility for preparing what will have to be a set of integrated briefs for all the service suppliers. In the end, the advertiser will benefit (or suffer) from the consequences of the advertising and so (as argued in Chapter 11) must take full responsibility for preparing the brief.

THE PLANNING SEQUENCE

The starting point for the advertiser should be a business plan for the coming financial year which specifies (among other things) the corporate and financial objectives, the resources available to achieve them, and the planning assumptions for the business environment in which this is expected to take place (see Chapters 1, 3 and 5).

From these can be developed integrated plans for each part of the business, including marketing, which specify the role each must play in achieving the objectives, and their allocated budgets.

By this stage, basics should have been agreed such as a Market Appreciation with forecasts; quantified targets for sales volume, value and profitability; a precise definition of the target market, and how the (extra) sales will come from them; and an outline marketing strategy to achieve the business objective within the set budget in the expected competitive climate.

GETTING THE CONTENT RIGHT

The briefing to the advertising agency (and all other outside suppliers) should therefore start by making available the Market Appreciation, Objectives and Strategy. If they are to do their job well, the suppliers should necessarily be capable of assimilating these data and keeping them confidential. Each should then be assigned the (unique) role which their work will play, how much money will be available for it, its timing, any essential corporate or market constraints, and the criteria by which the effects will be judged.

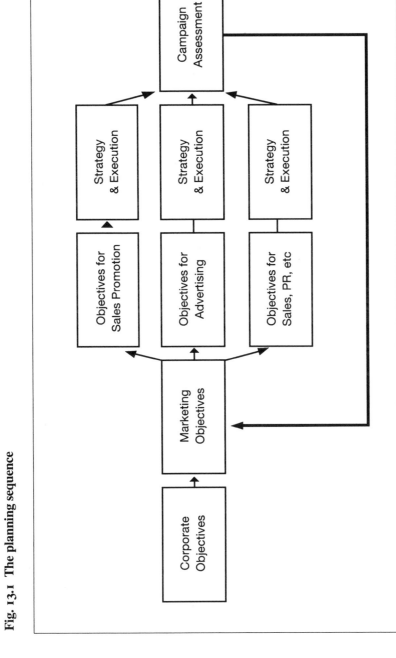

Fig. 13.1 The planning sequence

Fig. 13.2 The advertising brief

- Market appreciation and forecasts; how will the business climate develop in the next year/three/five years? What changes are expected in customer demand and the competition?
- Marketing objectives and strategy: quantified targets for sales, price, profit; targets, definition of target market; outline marketing strategy and budget.
- Product positioning: what is the key customer need, and how does the product satisfy it? (that is: what is the advertiser selling, and what is the customer buying?)
- What is the role of advertising in achieving the marketing objectives? How is that unique to advertising? (that is: why advertise?)
- The advertising budget (is that an increase or decrease, absolutely and as percentage of target sales?)
- Target audience (same as target market, or with restrictions or emphases?)
- What is to be communicated (that is: product benefits, end-uses, images, attitudes etc)? Is that a reinforcement or a change?
- Time constraints, co-ordination with other activity, other factors to be taken into account.
- How will the effects of advertising be evaluated? When, by whom and on what grounds will proposed advertising be approved?

Of greatest importance to effective advertising are clear, consistent, detailed statements of:

a) Target Audience: to whom the advertising is to be aimed (target companies and the key members of their DMUs, specifying as appropriate authorisers, specifiers, specialist advisers, buyers, users and any others who influence the decision).

b) Positioning: what the product category is used for and the need it satisfies, the reasons why they will want to buy our brand rather than the competition.

c) Desired Corporate Image: how this product fits in with the totality of the advertiser's operations, with the implied benefits and constraints.

Such a brief, once developed and agreed, should be robust enough to need little more than fine-tuning from year to year as the market develops. Frequent fundamental revisions to advertising content (unless demanded by *major* changes in the marketplace) confuse the buyers, weaken the product image and undermine brand loyalty. Any substantial change in strategy, particularly at short notice, is a traumatic and expensive event, not to be undertaken lightly.

COMMUNICATING THE BRIEF

Finally, it is important to communicate the brief. Ultimate responsibility again lies with the advertiser, but wise clients hold planning discussions with their agencies early enough for their views to affect the outcome. After all (as argued in Chapter 11), an agency with a deep concern for the business of a wide spectrum of clients may well have useful input to planning assumptions, and can act as an informed 'second opinion' on the viability of targets and alternative strategies. Further, an agency which has been consulted will have a better understanding of the background to their brief, a stronger belief in its validity, and a deeper commitment to its fulfilment.

At the least, the agency's Annual Briefing should be taken seriously. A written document is essential for continued reference, but first it should be presented and discussed. At this meeting, the client's staff whom the agency regularly contact should be supported at senior level (for example, by the Marketing Director); while the full agency team (including not just the account managers but also representatives of creative, media, research, print and other departments as appropriate) should be led by top agency management. Only in this way can it be ensured that the agency fully understands the brief and its importance, and that both sides at all levels are committed to its execution.

Half-hearted or imprecise briefs lead to uncreative and irrelevant executions, or to subsequent arbitrary modifications. In the long run the profits of both agency and client will suffer. A clear, relevant, well-communicated brief, especially if it can be expected to be robust enough to hold through most circumstances that are likely to arise, will act as a stimulus and guide to produce the kind of advertising which will be cost-effective in its own right, and also help support the rest of the marketing mix. Campaigns based on such briefs can even improve their effectiveness year by year!

14

INTEGRATION: HOW TO GET THE CAMPAIGN TACTICS RIGHT

Integrating the whole campaign with the lead activity will multiply the effects of the expenditure

STRATEGIC MARKETING

Part A of this book dealt with the strategic issues of a campaign. First, getting to know who your present and potential customers are and how they take their decisions, and selecting from them the key targets for sales in terms of companies and decision takers.

Second, agreeing specific and quantified business goals for all activities, which can and will be adhered to in all but the most dire of unforeseen emergencies. Such business goals imply that the level of activity necessary to achieve them can and will be funded, and if successful will generate an acceptable level of profit. This is a rational way of ensuring that an annual target for sales will be realistic, and greatly reduce the risks of a major and traumatic revision of the budget during the financial year.

Third, identifying the role of marketing (and other departments) in achieving these goals: in particular the channels by which the key customers can be reached and the most persuasive sales message to communicate to them.

Fourth, setting out those mandatory elements of the corporate image and house-styling which will not change from year to year (the 'packaging' by which the company will be recognised by the customers and the business community generally).

These four areas of decision by top management form the basis of a plan for all business activity, including marketing. If this plan is communicated to all decision takers within the company and to all outside agencies and suppliers, then the product and associated services, its pricing, distribution system, and all contacts with or messages to the customers will reinforce each other, and consequently improve the corporate reputation of the supplier. It will also help to ensure consistency of effort from year to year.

SUCCESSFUL CAMPAIGN TACTICS

Part B of the book has dealt with the way in which an effective marketing campaign can be developed. The starting point after agreeing the strategic issues (which affect all company activity not just marketing) is to single out a 'lead activity': the marketing communications (marcoms) technique whose success will most influence the outcome of the campaign. This is most likely to be chosen from media advertising, direct response, sales promotion, or public relations.

Whichever is chosen, it will be fundamental to the success of the campaign that all other techniques to be used must incorporate and include the theme of the lead activity. If each activity is allowed to develop in isolation, each will almost certainly come up with a different theme. These may well be equally 'creative' and successful for their technique if used on their own, but if executed independently will lose all synergy, run the risk of creating confusion in the marketplace and at worst might even reduce the effectiveness of the campaign as a whole.

The strategic plan and the campaign theme together form the brief for those who have to develop and execute the campaign, both internal marketing staff and outside agencies and suppliers. All such people must be made to work to the same brief, and (as described in Chapter 13) the best way of ensuring this is at a face-to-face meeting at which the full briefing documents are presented and discussed.

At this meeting, marketing management must identify the lead technique and specify the separate (and ideally unique) role of it and of each other planned activity in achieving the overall marketing objectives. They must also state how the success or otherwise of each activity will be evaluated, and who is responsible for doing the evaluating.

Finally, a timetable needs to be set up and agreed for development of each part of the campaign. This should include at least two dates for liaison, at which all those present at the initial briefing reassemble, to check that activity so far is on brief and is 'playing the same tune'. It is usually most helpful if the first liaison meeting is timed when campaign plans are complete but before the more expensive execution stage is commissioned; and the second when the campaign material is almost all ready to run, but there is still time to make minor adjustments economically.

Marketing management must be ruthless in bringing back into line any part of the operation which does not adhere to the agreed common direction, message or corporate image. There may be pressure from suppliers to get agreement for a 'highly creative idea' which needs modification to the brief after the event to accommodate it. This should always be resisted: if it is not on brief, it is not part of the campaign!

EVALUATION AND FEED-BACK

Creating and executing the elements of a campaign is the job of qualified specialists. These specialised tasks will include creative and media planning, production, research, public relations, promotional sourcing, compiling and managing databases and so on. Some of these tasks will be carried out in-house by staff members, but most marketing companies will use a very wide range of techniques and skills (some of them only intermittently) and must therefore rely on outside agencies, suppliers or consultants as appropriate.

Each should be chosen because they have the depth of skill, breadth of experience, adequate resources and above all the 'creativity' to plan and carry out their tasks. The best way of ensuring outside agencies do a good job is to brief them thoroughly, set firm but realistic budgets and timetables, and then to let them get on with it.

However, marketing management need (and have the right to ask for!) reassurance, before incurring any major expenditure, that the proposed activity is on brief, within budget, and likely to achieve its agreed objectives. The agencies and suppliers concerned should be prepared to back their recommendations with such reassurance expressed as concretely as practicable. Reliable ways of doing this include codified past experience, pre-tests with customers using rough materials, and (especially where large sums of money are at risk) small-scale market tests.

Further, marketing management (not the agencies) are ultimately responsible for evaluating the effectiveness and cost-effectiveness against the agreed objectives of the campaign as a whole and of its component activities. This cannot be done from scratch after the event, and (as discussed in Chapter 12) requires that a monitoring system is in place before the campaign starts, to supply baselines and regular measurements against pre-set action standards.

The results should be reviewed with all agencies and suppliers at first hand and at regular intervals. If something is going wrong they should be among the first to know, and preferably in time to do something about it. The purpose of the reviews should not be to allocate blame for failures; but rather to identify strengths and weaknesses in the elements of the campaign individually or in their integration. This will facilitate continuous fine tuning, and can be incorporated in future briefings so that the campaign will grow more effective or efficient year by year.

As emphasised in Chapter 13, the most frequent causes of failure in marketing campaigns arise at the briefing stage. The most frequent effect of such failure is a lack of integration between each of the different activities and of all of them with the corporate business plan. Consequently, customers are confused with conflicting messages, the corporate and product images become indistinct, and tactical sales opportunities get overlooked.

By contrast, a properly integrated campaign generates synergy whereby different activities reinforce each other and cover all opportunities with no loopholes. This provides cash benefits: in the short term better sales at higher margins; and in the longer term a loyal customer base and a strong corporate image, both assets which translate into 'goodwill', a capital asset on the balance sheet.

Fig. 14.1 Ten 'Golden Rules' for orchestrating and integrating all the elements of a campaign against the marketing goals

A: Marketing strategy (to be agreed before briefing internal marketing staff, outside agencies and other suppliers)

1   Set specific objectives for marketing communications to achieve, based on the marketing goals required by your company business plan.

2   Review the decision making process in your market in order to identify the key target audiences; to identify the best techniques and media to reach them effectively; and to help develop the most persuasive selling message.

3   Set out the common elements required for corporate image and house style.

B: Campaign tactics (to develop a campaign most likely to meet the objectives)

4   Single out the lead activity – the one whose success will most influence the outcome of the campaign. Make it fundamental to the campaign that all other activities must incorporate and reflect the creative theme of the lead activity.

5   Give all marketing staff, marketing communications agencies and other suppliers the same full briefing – and ideally do it at a single meeting with everyone in attendance.

6   Within this briefing clearly define the (ideally unique) role to be played by each marketing activity in achieving the overall objectives, and specify how each will be evaluated.

7   Set up a campaign development timetable, with at least two liaison dates built in, to ensure that all agencies and suppliers are on brief and are playing the same tune.

C: Evaluation and feed-back

8   Set up a monitoring system to evaluate the execution and effectiveness of the whole campaign and of each activity against its specific objectives. Review results with all agencies and suppliers at first hand.

9   Be ruthless in bringing back into line any part of the campaign which does not adopt the agreed common direction, message and corporate image, for whatever reason.

10 Highlight any weaknesses encountered in the integration of all the individual elements developed for the campaign, and identify how it can be made more effective in future.

Part C

SPECIAL TECHNIQUES AND SITUATIONS

15

STIMULATING SUCCESSFUL DIRECT RESPONSE

Advertising that can be demonstrated to make money, even in the short term

DEFINITION OF DIRECT MARKETING

Direct Response is one of the fastest growing areas of business marketing: originally among companies who require a constant stream of new leads 'off the page' for their salesforces, and later among business-results companies who have to generate all their sales more economically.

Direct Response can be defined as: *marketing communications aimed at stimulating an immediate response: such as a sales lead, enquiry or actual sale directly from customer to supplier.*

This chapter summarises first-hand experience of how Direct Response can be used most cost-effectively by marketers aiming at business markets.

BUSINESS MARKETS

As said in the Introduction, much of the theory of marketing was first developed in the context of consumer goods and services. Business-to-business marketers can benefit from this experience, but only if the differences between domestic and industrial buying decisions are clearly understood.

In contrast with consumer markets, where potential buyers are numbered in millions, in most industrial markets the number of businesses likely to buy a particular good or service will be numbered only in thousands; and following the '80:20 rule', a very high proportion of actual sales will come from a small proportion of this total. Further, and again in contrast with consumer markets, within each large customer business, the DMU is likely to be multi-layered, extending beyond the Purchasing Department to people at several levels in other departments with the power to influence the decision positively or negatively.

THE OPPORTUNITY

This provides the opportunity of building up and maintaining lists, not only of past and potential customer companies, but also the names and job titles of those who purchase, specify, advise, authorise and use the product. In many cases a few thousand (even a few hundred) names will cover a high proportion of sales.

In such circumstances, Direct Response can be one of the most powerful and cost-effective marketing techniques: to build lists, to generate sales leads, to pre-sell a call by the salesforce and actually to create sales.

The Direct Response technique, partly because of the success of its pioneers, partly because of recent developments in information technology, has become much larger and consequently offers business marketers more problems as well as new opportunities.

DIRECT RESPONSE AS A MARKETING TECHNIQUE

Direct Response is not a synonym for Direct Mail, although mail is currently by far the most usual Direct Response medium. Direct Responses have also been successfully stimulated by press advertising, literature, telephone, on-line videotex and even TV.

Direct Response contrasts with 'image' advertising. Most of the latter attempts to communicate information, which is intended to encourage favourable attitudes to the product or its supplier, so that the potential customer is more likely to choose it when buying. (Incidentally, mail can be used as a supporting medium in an image campaign, but need not necessarily ask for specific response.)

Because advertising is only one of many independent factors which influence a sale, quantification of the effectiveness of image advertising is an exacting task, usually requiring tracking studies of customer usage and attitudes followed by sophisticated analysis.

By contrast, the effectiveness of Direct Response activity is (at least at the basic level) very simple to measure. By definition, every Direct Response advertisement or mailing asks for specific action from its target. These actions are identifiable, and so the results of each operation can readily be tracked.

By simple accountancy, its cost-effectiveness against its objectives (and perhaps in comparison with other activities) can then be assessed. Further, experimentation can be used to determine which elements in the campaign are more and less cost-efficient. By systematically changing the variables (offer, response device, layout, headline, medium or list) and subjecting the outcome to rigorous and objective statistical analysis, the cost per contact or per unit sale can be evaluated and consistently reduced. The secret is to establish a 'creative control' (that is, the most effective approach tried so far), and a 'media/list control', and then to keep testing to beat the controls. There are many examples of progressive and sometimes dramatic increases in effectiveness over a period of time.

Experience of a wide range of approaches has led to some general conclusions about making a success of Direct Response Marketing to business audiences.

ROLE OF DIRECT RESPONSE IN THE MARKETING MIX

Because of the complexities of the typical DMU, business-to-business marketing is usually a more complex process than for most consumer products. No single technique is likely to cover all needs on its own.

Personal selling frequently takes the lion's share of the marketing budget, but the average cost of a sales call is now so high (over £200 in the UK and double that across Europe as a whole; see Fig. 18.2) that it is vital to ensure that each call is cost-effective. This means that each face-to-face visit has to be to the right person, at the right time, and have maximum effect.

Other supporting marketing techniques are needed to ensure this: media advertising, public relations, print, trade fairs and exhibitions, sponsorship, sales promotions and direct mail. The last has three useful supporting roles (in addition to identifying prospects):

- to pre-sell a personal call
- to cover members of the DMU who cannot be contacted personally
- to follow up a call, proposal or presentation.

When the number of potential customers is small, and the average order is substantial, the 'affordable cost of sale' per customer is usually quite large. Even allowing for reasonable sales force and corporate promotion costs, a margin can be found for a campaign of mailings. This technique can be tightly targeted, is flexible, and has a relatively low cost per unit, and so can be run at a high quality, be fully personalised and appropriately timed.

When the average order is small, regular personal selling becomes too expensive, making telephone and mail the *only* cost-effective techniques of closing a sale.

CORPORATE IMAGE AS A PRE-SELLING TECHNIQUE

Much direct mail arrives 'cold' to a prospect who has no particular need for the product at the time (but who may have one at a later date), and who may have little awareness of the company concerned. Research has shown that customers are far more likely to buy from a supplier they know well, and whom they believe to be reputable.

Advertising should be used to build and maintain a favourable 'corporate image' for a company. Once built, quite low sums are enough to maintain this image provided they are spent regularly and consistently. Additional weight can then be added in support of sales drive or new product launches (and to counteract crises or adverse publicity, although that is another story, told in Chapter 6).

Experience also shows that personal and telephone sales calls and direct mailings are almost always more effective if pre-sold by means of media advertising in the business or relevant technical press.

INFORMATION TECHNOLOGY AND LIST-BUILDING

The most valuable marketing tool for any business-to-business supplier is a comprehensive list of potential buyers and those who influence them: by name, company and job title. Compiling such a list and keeping it up-to-date is a lengthy and usually expensive process.

Several methods must be used, starting with customers and other existing contacts: from the sales force, trade fairs and conferences, plus personal and telephone callers. All company staff who ever meet outsiders should be trained to record as much relevant information as possible, and to pass it on to the company database. A special record sheet for this purpose may help.

This basic list must be supplemented. Conventional sources for prospects are trade directories and brokers with ready-made lists. These vary in relevance, accuracy, comprehensiveness and up-to-dateness, and the best are often expensive. Not all will offer individual names within companies (except perhaps for CEOs or Company Secretaries), and since the DMU will vary from product to product, few will be comprehensive.

More pro-active methods to identify prospects include couponed advertising. This should make an offer such as a booklet or technical guide, or an invitation to a seminar, presentation or trade show. These offers should be designed to be of great interest to potentials but to nobody else.

By definition, all Direct Response material must emphasise that the recipient should respond, and will benefit by so doing. It must also make as clear and easy as possible *how* to respond: for instance, supply printed 'freepost' envelopes, coupons large enough to write on, suggest 'just attach your business card' or 'tick the items of interest'. And then include a further offer in the material you send in response to the first response, thereby building a dialogue.

Many technical journals have a 'response card' system to facilitate response, and 'controlled circulation' publications have distribution lists which are accurate, named and specific. Mailing out packs of returnable 'product cards' has gained surprisingly good response.

All respondents to such activities should be followed up (preferably by telephone) to determine a few objective facts about each and a subjective view of their potential. 'Merge–purge' programmes must be used regularly to clean out overlap between different sources. This saves money in duplicated effort, but most importantly avoids the 'turn-off' effect of inundating a prospect with multiple copies of the same material.

Frequent up-dating is vital. A substantial proportion (assume at least 20 per cent) of the names on any list are likely to have changed job or location or company within 12 months of its compilation. Mailed material or personal contacts addressed to the previous incumbent of a job, or which fail to acknowledge the target's latest promotion, or indeed which are addressed to a job title only, cause as much ill-will as a misspelled personal or company name. With today's computer software, mailings beginning 'Dear Sir or Madam' are no longer necessary, and indeed look perfunctory. Good feed-back systems help, and company Information Departments who scan the customers' trade press can look out for news of mergers, moves and promotions.

THE 'GOLDEN RULES' FOR SUCCESS

Nothing 'always' works, and the market constantly changes. Nevertheless, there is no need for each newcomer to Direct Marketing to invent the wheel expensively from scratch. Experience teaches some 'golden rules' which help to ensure effectiveness. Here are seven:

Golden rule 1

Set quantified action standards before starting. In particular, set targets for cost-per-sale, per sales lead or per reply.

Make them realistic, so that a successful campaign can be expected to achieve them, and to be cost-effective when it does so. Do the sums *before* starting the exercise: they may show that the targets first set are unachievably high or unrealistically low.

Golden rule 2

Test and re-test everything to beat the 'controls'. If (as a matter of policy) you never stop testing, you will always continue to improve your performance. Test systematically: product, offer, media, creative approach.

For example, research has shown that technicians are hesitant to cut coupons from the publications they keep for reference. A test of a reply paid card insert increased response 19-fold. In another example, simplification of a complex mailing generated higher response, and cost less to produce!

Golden rule 3

Combine winning elements. The biggest gains in cost-efficiency are made by the multiple effect of more than one improvement, such as combining advertising with direct mail.

In one case, a company's complete customer application form out-performed a simple coupon by 50 per cent. When this was enhanced by a better headline and a new media plan, cost-per-sale was reduced by a massive 75 per cent.

Golden rule 4

Analyse objectively and ruthlessly. In Direct Response there is no room for an emotional or subjective opinion. Testing must be used to find the objective answer.

Know your figures, never fudge them. There is a great deal of statistical theory available to help you decide how much weight to put on your conclusions, and how to design experiments which will produce reliable data in the first place.

The cost accountancy must be done thoroughly. Do not miss the 'hidden costs' (such as staff time and fulfilment), often overlooked when making comparisons between one approach and another.

Golden rule 5

Build a quality database. Most lists of existing customers are built for invoicing, not selling. Make sure all the facts you know are attached to the names and addresses: who buys most often, most different products, in largest quantities, for which purposes? Who places the order, who takes the decision and who gives advice?

Add potential buyers by merging names from other lists, from couponed advertising, from reading the trade press, from controlled circulation publications, by recording contacts at trade fairs and so on. Keep the lists as clean, up-to-date, and comprehensive as possible. 'Database Marketing' has moved on from being the latest buzzword to the driving force in the Direct Response business (see Chapter 16)!

Note that past customers are the best prospects, both to re-order and to act as 'word-of-mouth' advertising for you. For this group, it is particularly easy to keep in touch, and give the kind of information they might want to pass on. Costs of regular mailings will be low.

One high-tech company has built a world-wide list 17 000 strong, of virtually all specifiers, influencers and decision takers in their field. Three to four times a year they are sent a highly authoritative and exclusive journal, and have to fill in each year a detailed request form to remain on the circulation list.

Modern computer technology will allow you to 'personalise' your contacts, so that recipients are sent only what you know to be relevant to their needs. This improves response, reduces the cost to you and minimises irritation to the customers.

Golden rule 6

Ensure fast and accurate fulfilment first. Research shows, year after year, that:

- fulfilment is the main source of both satisfaction and dissatis-faction among customers
- successful Direct Response marketers build their business on looking after their customers
- central to good fulfilment is speed of response. Your adver-tisements or mailings have raised their interest, take them to the next step before this has cooled off!

Golden rule 7

Be creative, look for the break-through. Tried and tested ideas (which can be combined!) include:

- making a promise in the headline
- making an offer to tempt a reply (for example, '70 new tricks to teach your computer!')
- be informative, and interesting (for example, technical guides)
- use problem/solution, to flag the customers you can really help
- be inventive, offer the unexpected (for example, a mousetrap to a computer firm, a can of 'instant finance' from a loan company to motor dealers)
- be topical (for example, a Valentine's Day Card that arrives on February 14th).

SUMMARY

Direct Response is the one marketing technique which permits quick and accurate evaluation. It can be used for many objectives, from generating a mailing list through pre-selling a personal approach to pulling actual sales.

Success depends on constant and objective testing and evaluating alternative creative ideas. Use computers thoughtfully to permit personalisation, and matching promotion to recipient in more motivating and cost-effective ways than ever.

Use advertisements to build lists and identify leads. Use mail to follow up and build repeat business. Always evaluate everything!

16

EFFECTIVE DATABASE MARKETING

How to start a dialogue with your customers

BACKGROUND

'Database marketing' has been much 'hyped' and mysticised over the last few years while establishing its place in the lexicon of marketing jargon. It is a phrase capable of striking unjustifiable fear into the hearts of even hardened and experienced marketers. In fact, database marketing is no more than a cost-effective method of communicating regularly with your market with the objective of improving the bottom line.

Database marketing uses modern technology to do what good salespeople have always done; namely, to keep track of customers and prospects and create a marketing edge by building a dialogue with them.

Fig. 16.1 shows how this process has evolved from reliance on human memory, through paper-based systems to the use of computer technology. Not too long ago, the Kardex type of card file was king. Customer records, visits, contacts and buying history were held on simple cards, usually jealously guarded by the salesperson concerned!

Computing entered the scene through 'transactional databases': an impressive way of saying that the accounts department was the driving force. The objective was to invoice people, chase

Fig. 16.1 The history of databases

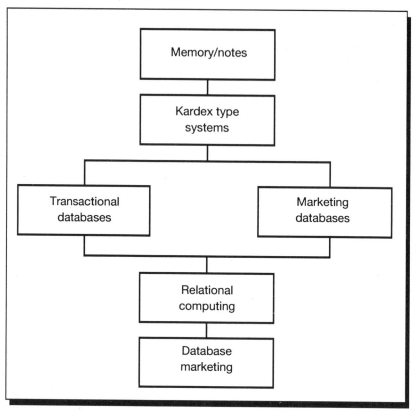

payments and provide management reports more efficiently. In parallel, but somewhat later, other departments began to receive some of the benefits – first distribution, then production, finally marketing. Even today, in most companies, that is as far as things have progressed. The marketing database cannot communicate effectively with other company systems.

Enter the latest development: the 'relational database'. This is a system where the whole computing network is so designed that any one database can tap into, link with and use any other database in the system. This interaction can mean for example that when a sale is recorded, invoicing is processed automatically, management accounts are up-dated, delivery instructions produced and stockholding records adjusted, average sales figures are recalculated by product and type, including moving annual totals and trends, projections of future sales and manufacturing planning amended to reflect the most up-to-date information.

IMPACT ON MARKETING

There is some very impressive hardware, some extremely innovative software and some complex systems integration involved in such systems. Fortunately, there are hundreds of companies and thousands of people in the market who understand such things, to whom the marketer can turn in time of need.

What is of fundamental interest is the choice of marketing options which such databases make available: from customer profiling to sales forecasting, from cross-selling to customer-retention programmes. Some examples of effective usage follow:

a: Profiling

An analysis of the database identifies, for example, that product 'A' is purchased mainly by a certain type of buyer. The buyer or customer can be described in detail (perhaps in demographic and lifestyle terms for a consumer product or industry type, job function and background for a business-to-business product). We can now seek out other people of the same type and produce highly targeted direct mail led with a proposition tailored to that particular audience.

b: Cross-selling

Past sales history identifies that buyers of product 'B' are also likely to have a need for product 'C'. Yet, actual sales of product 'C' to these people are relatively low. Again, we can identify a tightly targeted segment of prospects who can be approached cost-effectively.

c: Customer retention

Where a product has a predictable average life or perhaps a fixed end-of-contract date, we risk losing that client at the point of repurchase or renewal. A good database can flag such dates at a given period in advance enabling the marketer to offer attractive terms, reinforce brand values, emphasise specific customer needs, in order to close the sale long before the client begins to consider competitive offerings.

d: Profitability assessment

The right database structure allows the profitability of each customer to be assessed: both short-term and long-term. This is a particularly valuable facility which can have a major impact on marketing.

Without the database, the best that is likely to be known is that it costs a certain amount to generate a lead and close a sale. The cost of each sale is compared with the profit from it to establish the viability of that particular part of the marketing programme. Yet, this can be a dangerously myopic view. If a typical customer stays with the company for 'X' years, making on average 'Y' purchases generating 'Z' profit, we have a much more meaningful measure of how much we can afford to invest in winning that business.

Thus, marketing activity which at first glance seems to be 'too expensive' can in fact be highly cost-efficient when 'lifetime value' of the customer is measured. Indeed, once the customer has been won, the database can be used to measure fall-out rate and to detect danger points so that action can be taken to beat the targets by minimising loss.

PREDICTING RESULTS

When we know and understand the response of our market to a particular promotional activity, we have an invaluable grasp of what works effectively with a given segment of our audience.

We are in a position to 'profile' that audience and then identify non-customers who share the same characteristics. If the statistical work is done properly, not only can we be confident that the same approach will work, but we will also be able to predict with a high degree of accuracy the sales results which will be achieved.

Note that computing power does not make any of these things possible. It simply does them faster. It turns a long and tedious manual and paperwork exercise into a fast and cost-effective process. Indeed, whilst it does not make any of the options possible, it may well make them viable for the first time.

MAKING IT HAPPEN

Fig. 16.2 outlines the key stages moving into database marketing.

Fig. 16.2 Developing a database

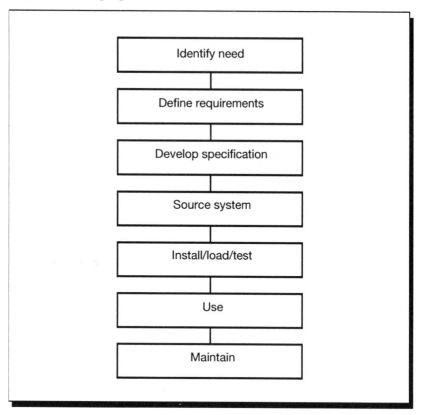

a: Identify need

Embarking on database marketing implies a direct cost and a substantial indirect cost in management time. It is wise, right at square one, to decide whether there is real benefit for the company to be gained from the investment.

In a market with a very small number of easily identified customers, it may be that the salesforce is in very regular contact with everyone who can influence a sale of the company's products. In a small company, there may not be the ability to make use of a sophisticated database system.

In the former case, paper-based systems may be adequate for the company's needs. In the latter, the optimum solution may be a relatively simple sales and marketing software package readily available off-the-shelf at moderate cost.

b: Define requirements

If the need does exist, the next stage is to identify what you want the database to do. Forget the technicalities; concentrate on the applications you can foresee:

- what will go on the database: customer firms, prospects, lapsed customers? How do you wish them to be identified: by size, by purchase pattern, geographically, by industry, by end-user category?
- how many records will be kept: in each category and in total?
- what level of information do you wish to hold on each member of the customer's DMU: name, address, telephone, fax, job title, purchasing history, contact dates, birthday, football team?
- what sorts of analyses will you require: sales by industry or technology, by product within region, correlations of buying patterns?
- what forms of output will be used: reports, labels, personalised letters?

It will pay at this early stage to brainstorm every conceivable use the company might make of the database, to produce an 'ideal' list of requirements. In practice, this may have to be curtailed at a later stage on cost grounds!

A key corporate decision to be faced at this point is whether the database will be stand-alone or relational. If it is to be fully integrated with all company systems, you will inevitably face longer lead time to operation, more complex systems development and much higher cost; but ideas which could have been built in almost free-of-charge at the beginning are likely to be costly or even impracticable at a later stage.

c: Specifying and sourcing the system

This is a topic where expert advice is well worth its cost. A specialist consultant will turn the client requirements into a target system specification and, in many cases, will be able to recommend a ready-made package of hardware, software and systems integration which will meet the specification.

d: Install, load and test

Installation and testing can be left to the experts but the question of loading the system raises important issues for the marketer.

Almost certainly, current client files will not hold information either in the depth or format required to meet the needs which you have defined. Records on the accounts database, for example, will probably have only a financial contact named and may even have an unhelpful address if the client's accounts department is centralised away from their buying points.

Your customer records will probably lack a great deal of the company and staff data which you have identified as being needed. However, you may well have some of the relevant information in other departmental files. How will you access and format it to load on the database? Do you propose to start afresh with sales information or to track back through your existing systems to build a picture of purchasing history?

How will you fill the gaps which are left? Will you cross-profile with market data (perhaps through syndicated research systems such as PIMS or ACORN)? Can you use the lists of controlled circulation publications? Can you fill any gaps through telephone research? All of this takes time and costs money: which needs to be taken into account. Again, a good specialist can advise.

Finally, when you have the information, who will physically sit down and load all of these records onto the system? What checking process will you use to ensure the loading is totally accurate?

e: Use and maintain

Eventually, the glorious day will dawn when you can mail all red-headed process engineers working in companies located in postal code RG and who purchased product 'X' between 12 and 18 months ago! A superb facility to target clearly defined customer and prospect groups.

But how will you know they have not all moved jobs since you loaded the database? Keeping any database up-to-date is perhaps the most exacting part of the process. Commercially available lists are updated by a range of techniques from simply registering mailings returned as 'gone-aways' to tracking through electoral registers and full on-going telephone research.

It is critical that a rigorous system is put in place which provides a central control for keeping the database up-to-date and for capturing new data to expand the file. There are two routes to dealing with both loading and maintaining the database. They can be done in-house or sub-contracted to a specialist bureau. Take advice on the pros and cons of each.

Fig. 16.3 Typical relational database use

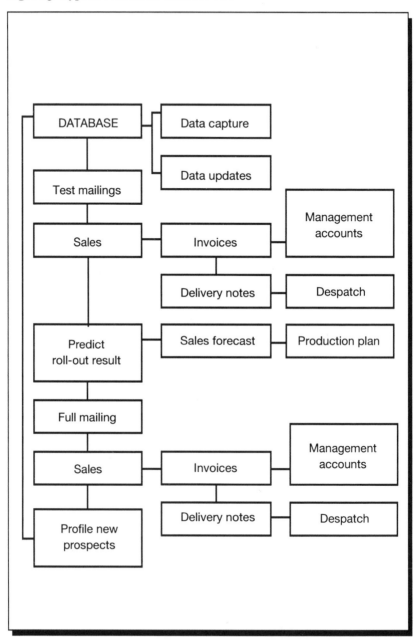

CONCLUSION

An effective database can be an excellent and highly cost-effective marketing tool. At one end of the scale it can be simply a more efficient way of holding records and communicating with the market, at the other it can be a core element in making the whole company more efficient by automating many of its processes and by bringing statistical objectivity to bear on fraught areas such as sales forecasting.

Adopting a database marketing approach is a major commitment of resources but it is not the mystical process it might seem. Help and expertise is readily available. And the competitive edge to be gained may be all-important to the company's future.

17

THE MOST NEGLECTED MARKETING TARGET: THE STAFF

The more people pushing it – the faster the marketing bandwagon will move!

ADVERTISING JUST SELLS TO CUSTOMERS – OR DOES IT?

Advertising for goods or services is aimed at present and potential customers, usually to persuade them to switch their regular purchases from their current supplier to the advertiser, or perhaps to encourage loyal buyers to buy the advertised product more often or use it in larger quantities. Effective advertising will indeed do this. But it does not act in isolation: advertising supports and is supported by the rest of the marketing mix.

In particular, it is often forgotten that advertising and other marketing communications have an effect on the *staff of the advertiser*. Yet, if each campaign is properly presented and explained to the salesforce, they will be motivated to sell more strongly and effectively to their customers. Indeed, if these customers are part of a distribution chain, they in turn will often be encouraged to stock more and to recommend the product to their own customers, just because it is being advertised.

Such planned reinforcement between personal and impersonal

customer communications can add substantially to the cost-effectiveness of the advertising and promotional budget. A campaign which is well 'merchandised' to salesforce and distributors can start to work even before the advertisements begin to appear.

Sales staff who are unsupported by advertising are inclined to major too often on price in their sales presentations and to offer too many discounts if they fear they will otherwise lose a sale. By contrast, when they know their customers have already been pre-sold by strong and effective advertising, salespeople tend to resist pressure to discount and instead stress the virtues of the product which they can be sure had attracted the buyer in the first place.

In other words, advertising will help to sell more and at better prices, if the advertiser's staff are familiar with it and believe in it (see Chapter 3).

THE SALES POTENTIAL OF STAFF TRAINING

To be fair, these days most salesforces are given formal training in customer care and their management take positive steps to brief them on how to reinforce the corporate image. This training can with benefit be extended to all 'front-line' staff who have direct contact with present and potential customers: technical advisers, media liaison staff, perhaps also the receptionists, security staff and switchboard.

Rather fewer companies take such trouble with the rest of their employees whose job does not bring them into everyday contact with the outside world. Yet some of them at all levels will know, be related to, travel to work with or otherwise meet regularly, the staff of customers, suppliers, competitors or the trade press. They may unwittingly (or sometimes even deliberately) spread undesirable or false information about their company; or they may be asked questions which they do not know how to answer.

More positively, all employees may at some time find themselves in a situation where they can enhance their employer's reputation. If they all know what to do, the company's marketing effort will be reinforced and its effectiveness can actually be multiplied.

INTERNAL AND EXTERNAL COMMUNICATIONS

The key points are: do the whole staff know where their company is heading? Do they know who the customers and desired potential customers are? Do they know what the customers are being told about the company and its products? Have they seen and had explained to them the advertising and other material which will be seen by the trade and the general public? A marketing strategy which is generally known to the staff will be effective because everyone's efforts will be co-ordinated to reinforce it. A marketing strategy known only to the marketing department is just another corporate secret.

For many companies the staff are the 'most neglected marketing target'. Internal communications should be as much a part of a corporate communications programme as external ones aimed at potential customers, suppliers, the media and government.

Experience shows it is well worth building activities into the planning cycle which keep the whole staff informed not only about their own job but about the total marketing effort. The usually quite modest expenditures needed to do this are likely to pay off handsomely.

HOW TO SET ABOUT IT

For a *small firm*, where there are perhaps only two layers of management between Board and rank-and-file, this ought not to be a problem. Communications should already be good, because all will know each other at least by sight, particularly where 'management by walking about' is the rule. Such firms anyway find it easy to have regular meetings of the whole staff, which form an excellent opportunity to give an airing to issues of company policy such as the marketing approach, particularly anything likely to be seen by the general public. Staff appreciate the courtesy of being shown their company's advertising before their family and neighbours see it; and if they have been told the strategy, they will be able to reinforce it.

For *larger firms* with hundreds of salespeople and perhaps thousands of other staff, located at several sites or at chains of outlets, such face-to-face briefings by top management are not practical, yet the need for them is actually greater. It is bad for public relations if customers get different responses at different locations. Several well-known distributors have been publicly pilloried by the UK Advertising Standards Authority because customers had been refused nationally advertised offers by branches which were not yet aware of them.

But how can larger firms set about this task? There are two basic approaches: personal and impersonal, which are complementary rather than substitutes for each other.

FACE-TO-FACE METHODS – THE MOST EFFECTIVE

Several chapters have reiterated that of all the techniques of business communication, by far the most effective is 'personal selling'. As the American media guru Marshall McLuhan first said, 'The Medium is the Message', and so the persuasive power of any message will be proportional to the standing of the messenger. For instance, a sales executive is far more likely to pass on to the customers 'what the top boss told me when we met' than something he or she read in the weekly departmental briefing letter. Anyone who has taken part in 'blockbuster' sales or dealer conferences knows their power to raise emotions which last long after everyone has returned to normal business life.

So while CEOs of giant corporations cannot gather their whole staff in one hall, it is highly motivating if as many as possible are regularly gathered to be complimented on their past performance from the very top and briefed about the problems and opportunities of the future, with the chance to comment and discuss in smaller groups with people more senior than those met during day-to-day work. As an indicator of the value of such gatherings, several companies with large franchised salesforces run annual conferences where the franchisees willingly pay their *own* money for the opportunity to meet the boss and to applaud each other's achievements.

The cost of conference venues limits the size and frequency of such gatherings. But the technologies of videotape, videodisc or even of video telephone can bring the boss's presence and all the latest news simultaneously to branch, region or departmental meetings. The words 'I want you to be the first to know . . .' can do much to raise the morale of the hearers. Senior local management can pre-sell and afterwards reinforce and localise the message.

Where money is regularly invested in sponsorship of sports and arts, opportunities can be created to extend the benefits beyond media coverage: namely to show staff and customers the 'company image in action'. The salesforce can entertain valued customers at 'our match' cheaply and without the drawback of having to negotiate sales. At the same event, the general staff can be offered the chance to 'support our team'. Besides gratitude for a good day out, loyalty to the team may spill over to its sponsor.

NON-PERSONAL TECHNIQUES – THE MOST ECONOMICAL

Costs may limit big staff gatherings to such major events as new product launches. Continuity should nevertheless be kept, and indeed these occasions can be reinforced and sustained effectively by lower key methods.

Even traditional 'Messages To All Staff' will gain higher attention value if they are circulated in the form of personal letters instead of just pinned to the bulletin board. Desk-top publishing software can give company newsletters much of the impact of a commercial magazine with the added bonus of personalisation.

Videotape of the company product demonstration films can have the advertising spliced into it, and if run continuously in the reception area will be seen not only by visitors but also by the staff, who should be encouraged to take a new look whenever the reel is updated.

When national advertising is used, staff will be able to make sure they see it if they have been told the schedule, and such a public showing ought to improve their self-image even more than an internal one.

For companies with very large and scattered work forces it may even be worthwhile to place advertising aimed primarily at employees. For example, it is believed that the otherwise notorious 'We're Getting There' campaign by British Rail was intended in part to exploit the authority of television to encourage BR station staff to take improving customer service more seriously. Companies with successful long-term Corporate Image campaigns (such as ICI and BP) may sometimes include within them advertisements intended to achieve internal objectives such as enhancing staff morale and improving quality of recruitment.

In these days when the vogue is for 're-engineering' a company, or otherwise drastically changing its corporate culture (for example by merger), it is essential to provide regular and personal communications with all staff to prevent anxiety and destructive rumour followed by the departure of key specialists for self-protection.

However, as with all marketing activity, an effective communication has to be two-way. Whichever techniques are used, the staff must have, and know about, a way to ask questions and put forward their own ideas.

THE BENEFITS

Companies gain a number of benefits when they take the trouble to develop an integrated programme of personal and non-personal communications to explain to their whole staff their marketing approach. Some of the benefits will be intangible, others will directly improve the bottom line.

First of all, the sales staff and their distributors will be enthused to sell harder and to get better prices. Further, all staff at some time or another have opportunities to support the sales effort, but can exploit them only if they know how, and if not may ignore or even hinder them. If all staff know about the marketing targets and are working in harmony to achieve them, the effectiveness of the formal external marketing activity (such as media advertising) will be greatly enhanced.

In addition, it is useful for senior management to have regular dialogue directly with their whole staff on a topic where both

Fig. 17.1 The neglected marketing target: the staff

The need:
- To ensure that all staff, particularly but not only those who meet the customers, know about the company's marketing objectives, and have seen the advertising.

The objectives:
- Regular briefing by top management (the more senior the better) on policy and strategy.
- Seeing everything aimed at the customers before they do.

The methods:
- Personal contact – powerful, but time-consuming, costly and not appropriate for very large numbers.
- Regional or departmental staff meetings run by local management supporting input from Head Office.
- Indirect methods – letters, news magazines, videos, media advertising, sponsorship activity.

The direct and indirect methods are not substitutes, they should all be used to reinforce each other.

The benefits:
- More enthusiastic personal selling efforts.
- Co-ordination of effort.
- Leverage on the marketing budget.
- A neutral channel of communication between management and staff.

The pay-off:
- Higher general levels of morale.
- Better sales at better prices.

have a non-adversarial interest (that is, improved sales and profits) and which can legitimately by-pass the normal chain of command and any formal negotiating mechanisms. Such a channel of communication, once open and accepted, can be used on occasion to help inform and educate the staff over a broader range of issues.

Finally, staff have a higher morale and consequently higher productivity, if they understand where their company is going and believe their bosses care enough to take them into confidence about it. Such companies tend to suffer less from damaging rumours, hostile jokes (about 'mushroom management' for instance), or even absenteeism.

This implies that top management would be wise to allocate reasonable time and modest amounts of money to achieve such objectives. Experiments can prove that an investment in internal communications can become progressively valued by the staff and increase significantly the cost-effectiveness of communication with customers.

18

THE 'EUROBUYER': MARKETING TO THE SINGLE MARKET

Think European, act local. Yes, but how do we do that?

INTRODUCTION

It is inevitable that from the 1990s onwards few businesses (except the very smallest) will be able to survive on sales in their home country alone. While this does not imply every business has to become world-wide in its operations, and indeed the announcement of the 'global village' in the 1970s has turned out to be a little premature, the world is coalescing into regional groups. A British business in the 1990s has to consider itself European and a Canadian business North American.

This chapter takes a European perspective. Most of what is published about the effects of the Single European Market (which many still refer to by its start date of '1992') relates to consumer goods and services, to the neglect of the equally important business-to-business sector. Success in the new Europe will depend on a good understanding of the differences between marketing to businesses and to domestic consumers, especially:

(i)   the relatively complex structure of customers' DMUs
(ii) the characteristic ways of doing business in each European

country, which will continue to differ for years, conceivably decades

(iii) the wider choice of communication channels through which business buying decisions can be influenced.

Even for a business already operating in Europe, implementing an effective marketing plan for the Single Market will probably demand changes in product offer, marketing mix, organisational structure and above all corporate attitudes, so as to profit from the new opportunities for integrated marketing communications campaigns. Much of this is still unknown territory, but this chapter collates current practical experience.

THE EURO DECISION MAKING UNIT

Earlier chapters have emphasised how all business-to-business marketing is about *interactive personal relationships* between the staffs of the supplier and of a relatively small number of identifiable present and potential customer firms. This is even more true when trade crosses frontiers.

Targeting companies who might buy a specific product or service should not be difficult, at least in those European countries where 'database-marketing' is already well-developed. The problem lies in identifying the key members of the DMU in each target company. Research suggests a DMU in Europe contains an average of nine people, varying by country between three and 20. It is interesting that more people are involved in a purchase from a local supplier than in a (presumably more risky) import. A significant proportion of firms also use outside financial or technical advisers in their buying process.

Experience suggests that the more important the decision, the larger the number of staff likely to be involved, with relocation,

Fig. 18.1 Average number of persons in a customer company involved in making purchasing decisions

Customer Country	Average	Supplier Country France	Germany	Sweden	Britain
France	10	20	7	5	7
Germany	8	7	15	6	5
Italy	6	8	4	3	8
Sweden	10	10	6	15	9
Britain	9	8	8	6	15
Average	9	11	8	7	9

Source: Turnbull & Valla: Strategies for International Industrial Advertising, Routledge, 1986.

changes in technology and other major capital transactions requiring wide consultation, and routine repurchases of a minor raw material and small items for personal use the least. Most executives have a set cash limit, above which they must obtain some form of official authorisation. Salespeople often connive with junior buyers to split large orders into a series of smaller ones each below the threshold.

EUROPEAN BUSINESS MANAGEMENT CULTURES

In a European context, these organisational factors will be complicated further by differing management styles. National differences in political, economic and industrial structure, education and just plain tradition have ensured that each country has its own ways of doing business, and commercial laws have tended to reinforce such differences. Law cannot in any case change basic national characteristics, and the trend to convergence inherent in the harmonisation of accounting practices and the mutual recognition of professional qualifications in the EU will take a long time to work through.

No one believes that all Scotsmen are mean or all Italians are excitable or all Belgians are bad drivers. Yet such national stereotypes have just enough basis in fact to be meaningful (indeed some night-club comedians make their living from them!). Similarly, it is the view of the author and many colleagues with international experience that there are also meaningful national stereotypes of companies. Someone who has to do business in an unfamiliar country may find them helpful, so long as they are not taken to apply in any individual case. The test of validity, of course, is not the stereotype of one's own country (which most people automatically reject) but of another which one knows well.

NATIONAL BUSINESS STEREOTYPES

For example, typical *German* companies (like American ones) are likely to have strong hierarchies and well-defined job functions. Managers are usually technically-qualified specialists with considerable authority over their specialisation. For most companies, planning is a formal process, so that relevant managers advise about their specific concerns, which advice top management then synthesise before taking the decisions. Suppliers' salesforces are expected to negotiate only with (powerful) Purchasing Departments, and will sour relationships if they attempt to go over their heads. The Specifiers in other departments (such as Engineers who have a particularly high status) have to be approached in other ways, such as trade fairs and advertising.

By contrast, in typical *Italian* organisations decisions tend to be taken informally by whoever is best able to implement them, usually after considerable personal contact and discussion.

Leadership is a respected art in Italy. Successful managers have to be flexible improvisers who ignore standard procedures whenever they get in the way of essentials. This leads to a strong temperamental aversion to forecasting and planning. Authority to influence and decide may not be delegated to holders of particular job titles, but to trusted individuals outside the apparent organisational structure, and even outside their own part of the organisation.

Inter-personal contact is therefore of very great importance in marketing in Italy. Finding the right decision taker is an art; but establishing rapport and commitment to a common purpose is vital for successful suppliers.

Because *Spain* had for years lagged economically behind Northern Europe, it has in the 1990s been able to sustain far higher growth rates, thereby moving from a largely agrarian to an industrial economy. But because of a shortage of local financial and managerial resources, much of the growth is being driven by American and German multi-nationals who are importing the organisational models of their parent companies.

Essentially Spanish businesses can be typified by a family firm where the owner rules benevolently but despotically over managers who carry out his or her personal instructions. Communications tend to be vertical and members of a 'team' may work independently with little mutual co-operation or interference. Suppliers may well find trouble in obtaining consent to a proposal; good personal relations are necessary to prevent middle management blocking all approaches, but anything important will probably have to be sent 'up the line' for final approval by 'El Jefe'.

Netherlands companies have since the 17th century been motivated in favour of international trade, because their home market is too small to support major industrial operations, and so build their businesses by competing in world markets. They claim that the Single Market is making less difference to them than to many of their competitors.

A typical *Dutch* company will show democratic leadership within a relatively highly structured organisation. Business relationships are often relaxed and informal. Dutch organisations tend to be lean, practical, obsessed with profitability, and use rigorous management systems designed to involve all levels in strategic thinking. Decisions are taken mainly through a series of formal and informal meetings, leading to a consensus to which all are then expected to adhere. Selling efforts therefore have to involve many personal contacts, which are often prolonged because members of the DMU wish to avoid conflict or definitive one-sided decisions.

Typical *British* companies show less polarisation. Specialist expertise is less highly regarded, and good managers are expected to be able to think and act as generalists. Decisions tend to come about by informal consensus developed in meetings, discussions and out-of-office contacts among middle managers, who then approach top management for ratification. Most activities in UK companies are heavily constrained by rigid financial plans, which are rarely modified except in times of crisis.

Suppliers to British companies need to get to know the various members of the DMU personally and informally. While the most professional managers prefer businesslike relationships, more business is still done in Britain than in other EU countries over the lunch table or on the golf course. Top management normally refuse routine contacts with suppliers, but are more likely to ratify proposals to buy from companies they know about (perhaps through 'corporate image' advertising in the business press).

THE EFFECTS OF THE SINGLE MARKET LEGISLATION

Business must continue to look forward to the prospect of a true Common Market with no frontiers and harmonised trading rules, which was envisaged in the 1957 Treaty of Rome and reiterated 30 years later in the Single European Act. When the Single Market officially opened in January 1993, some 25 per cent of the original package of necessary legislation had not yet been implemented across all 12 Member States, many new Directives on key topics (such as sales promotion) were still in prospect, and only limited progress had been made on the large and difficult but essential task of harmonising over 50 000 technical standards.

Hence, throughout the 1990s Euro-marketing will continue to face substantial local variations. Not just in the EU's legal requirements, but because any sensible definition of Europe for marketing purposes is likely to include both EU and EFTA states and probably some of those in the East which are not yet aligned. Further, and as already indicated, because of the widely different starting points in social, economic, industrial, logistic, climatic, educational and other basic characteristics of different countries and their business decision takers.

Yet eventual convergence at least of the business sector must be taken as inevitable, and the most successful operators will be those who plan for a Single Market and implement, ahead of the structural changes, as much as possible of their plans.

Suppliers or importers approaching Europe for the first time are fortunate to be able to tailor their offer and its marketing directly to the needs of the future. Most industrial companies in Europe already have a product range, production and distribution facilities, business from regular customers and an established corporate image, all of which may well vary from country to country for the (good) reasons discussed above. How do they get the promised economies of scale and other advantages from the Single Market, and how can the research business best help them?

THE BASIC DECISION:
THE PAN-EUROPEAN PRODUCT OFFER

To gain the benefits of a Single Europe, five basic decision areas must be reviewed from scratch, even by established and highly successful companies:

1 Define the marketing region

Europe has to be approached as a single operating area, and from an internal regional headquarters. The area defined need not coincide with European Union or other political boundaries. For example, if Greece or Denmark are too small, too 'different' or create logistic problems for a particular supplier, they need not be included; while Switzerland or Poland, if good prospects, need not be excluded (or almost as bad, treated as separate markets) just because they are not yet EU members. For some time to come, the variations between EU members will be as great as those between members and many non-members. Fragmentation of effort will diminish marketing power.

2 Define the marketing target

Create a census of companies throughout the region which have significant purchasing potential. This needs desk research of internal and external published data, supplemented by attendance at trade fairs and selective prospecting through telephone, mail, direct response advertising and personal contact. In making this search, national boundaries will be of little importance compared with market segments with common end-uses, types of production process or organisational structure which can be found *throughout* Europe.

3 Identify all members of the DMU in each target company

These should be listed by job title, function, degree of influence and ideally by name. This is a far more difficult and costly task, but could be said to be the highest priority for Market Research.

4 Specify the needs of and main channels of communication with individual members of the DMUs

5 Re-appraise the company's product offer

This should be done in the context of the resulting wider but more precise definition of the target market on a pan-European scale.

THE RELATIONSHIP OF MARKET RESEARCH TO RESEARCH & DEVELOPMENT

All authorities on the New Europe seem agreed on the need for more expenditure on R&D, where Europe has lagged badly behind the USA and more recently Japan. What is equally important is basic Market Research to direct such work into appropriate topics, followed by concept, prototype and price tests to make sure that its output is acceptable to the target customers. It is surprising that in many industrial firms in Europe, R&D and MR departments still do not automatically collaborate with each other.

A combination of R&D and MR will provide suppliers with enough up-to-date information about their offer to determine which of their current products fit target customers' future needs, which need modification, which must be phased out, and how important gaps can be filled. It must be kept in mind that the 'offer' of a good or service includes not just its specification, but also the price and terms of business, and the range of pre- and after-sales services normally expected by business customers.

Suppliers of consumer goods and services are currently agonising over the possibility of gaining huge economies of scale by developing 'Euro-brands' which fit generalised needs of large numbers of people throughout Europe instead of ranges of fragmented local or 'niche' brands.

This problem need not affect business marketers so much. In typical 'industrial' markets the large size of many orders, and a general need to negotiate individually terms of business and service, have meant that each sale has always been in effect a separate entity, even for a standardised core product. Indeed by adopting highly flexible, Computer-Aided-Design and Manufacture facilities for good economies of scale may be reached more often with quite small batch sizes. They will also enable suppliers to offer customers a higher degree of flexibility in specification and also Just-In-Time deliveries. Developing pan-European distribution and stock holding networks which do not have to depend on frontiers will facilitate important marketing benefits.

SELLING TO THE EURO-DMU

The traditional and most powerful method of selling to businesses has been by personal contact, although costs per call and per sale are high. The effectiveness of personal selling will not diminish, but for a pan-European operation, its costs will tend to increase. National sales forces have tended to be organised geographically, with relatively short travelling-time between calls. European sales forces will instead tend to specialise by customer type (perhaps by industry, process technology or organisational style), so that each salesperson's clientele will cover a wider geographical spread.

Consequently time and travelling costs per call will increase, and effectiveness may diminish unless the people concerned have good language skills. It is agreed that English is the most widely spoken business language in Europe, and is indeed mandatory in certain industries such as air travel, computers and pop music, and also among the higher echelons of British- or American-based multi-nationals. But on the factory floor and among customers without major international connections a monoglot salesperson may be at a disadvantage to a fluent competitor.

This will create pressure to use salesforces more efficiently and to concentrate personal calls by time and by place where they will be most effective. Other and cheaper means of communication with the potential customer's DMU will be used to deliver relevant information, to prepare for each call and to follow it up.

Given that at 1994 rates 1 ECU approximately equals \$1.20 or £0.80, Fig. 18.2 suggests that the cost per sale in the 1990s will average over ECU 3,000. If salesforce costs are budgeted at (say) 5 per cent of net sales value, an average order has to be nearly ECU 80 000 to make the sales effort cost-effective.

Fig. 18.2 Cost of a business-to-business sales call

Country	Cost per call $	Average number of calls per sale	Cost per sale $
Denmark	1,440	5.0	7,200
Italy	809	6.8	5,500
Sweden	710	6.4	4,540
France	772	5.4	4,170
Germany	678	6.1	4,140
Belgium	687	6.0	4,120
Switzerland	569	6.3	3,580
Netherlands	540	5.9	3,190
U.K.	304	5.3	1,610
Ireland	128	5.5	700
Average	640	6.0	3,840

Source: McGraw Hill, 1986

Anything which can reduce these costs by increasing the strike rate or size of order is worth investigation. For example, an activity which reduces the average number of calls per order from six to five, would justify a budget up to ECU 300 000 to target 1,000 customers.

Candidate activities are of course *marketing communications* techniques, especially advertising, direct mail, trade fairs and public relations. The right mix depends on what has to be communicated and the climate in which it has to act. Research demonstrates that this differs by country and, it can be speculated, by industry as well.

Trade magazines and professional journals are in regular use throughout Europe, and many have considerable authority with their readers. *Display Advertising* must therefore be the prime method both for pre-selling sales calls and for addressing those members of the DMU who are difficult to contact or whose degree of influence is insufficient to justify a personal call. A great deal of research has been carried out into how to make the most cost-effective use of the options of media selection, positioning, frequency, size and content.

Direct Mail (as described in Chapter 15) can be highly specific in its targeting, and can also be personalised and pre-tested. It is usually at its most cost-effective when used as a generator of sales leads or for pre-selling sales visits in conjunction with media advertising. Recent research by the European Direct Marketing Association demonstrates that Direct Marketing already accounts for nearly as high a share of marketing budgets across Europe as conventional 'image' advertising. The developments of Database Marketing and Tele-marketing will further speed the growth of this sector.

Trade Fairs and Exhibitions are big business, with some enormous and spectacular events. In Germany, most local companies both attend and take stands at their relevant *Messe*, while British competitors who are less impressed by the technique may be conspicuous by their absence.

Public Relations for commercial purposes are normally integrated with other promotional approaches. In selling to businesses, they are particularly helpful for dealing with technical advisers and specifiers who can be offered information-based items such as reports, scientific journals and seminars provided they are seen to be relevant and not just 'puffery' for the sponsor's products.

Suppliers will need *Market Research* among members of their target DMUs to determine what information each needs to help make up his or her mind about a purchase, the most authoritative technique to communicate it, and the most cost-effective medium by which it can be delivered. Of particular importance is information which will influence the early stages of decision-taking such as specification and which suppliers to approach, because personal contact may not then be practicable. It should be possible to demonstrate that the cost-savings from such information will pay for its collection many times over.

'THINKING EUROPE'

While many companies will need to make changes in their product offer and its marketing mix, if they are to succeed in the heavier competition of the 1990s, probably the most important modifications that European businesses will have to make will relate to corporate structures and above all, corporate attitudes.

Ever since the Single Europe Act was announced in 1987, all the pundits have said: 'Think Europe: act local.' What this means is: 'You are no longer a British/Spanish/Greek company trying to export your output all over Europe; you are in future a European company (which happens to locate its main production and administrative resources in Coventry/Madrid/Athens) marketing throughout its home territory.'

This has clear structural implications. A company which traditionally served a home market with strong regional variations would not split itself into autonomous subsidiaries for each separate sales region. It would naturally develop a comprehensive national strategy, but then take local market conditions and the local knowledge of its staff into account on implementation. A 'European-thinking' company will therefore set a common strategy for its total operations and for each brand throughout Europe, but will accept that modifications and adaptations may be necessary to make the most of local opportunities in customer behaviour or variations in trading conditions.

'Acting local' will be little different from what is happening now at national level. 'Thinking Europe' is a new and strategic concept for most companies, even for well-established multi-nationals.

MANAGEMENT STRUCTURES FOR A SINGLE EUROPE

If the potential of the Single Market is to be exploited, the organisational structures of many companies will have to change. Most multi-nationals are organised *vertically*, with responsibility for profits delegated within each separate country. In the past that has been the best way of maximising profitability and flexibility in each country; and local subsidiaries who consistently delivered the required ROI have usually enjoyed considerable autonomy.

In future, the whole of Europe must be seen as a single profit centre. This demands *horizontal* management structures, whereby individual managers are given responsibility for the total profit of each product and consequently the power to set targets and budgets throughout its 'home territory', Europe. Local management are then responsible only for tactical execution of the centrally set strategy. This structure enables resources to be allocated by area and by task where they will be most cost-effective.

In the past, horizontally structured multi-nationals have been seen as over-centralised and inflexible, but in a Single Europe they will be better placed to exploit the new opportunities than traditional vertically structured companies who will be hampered by the NIH syndrome (Not Invented Here – see Chapter 19).

Not that all the new Euro-product controllers need be located in one central Head Office. Group talents and alternative

Fig. 18.3 Multinational management structures

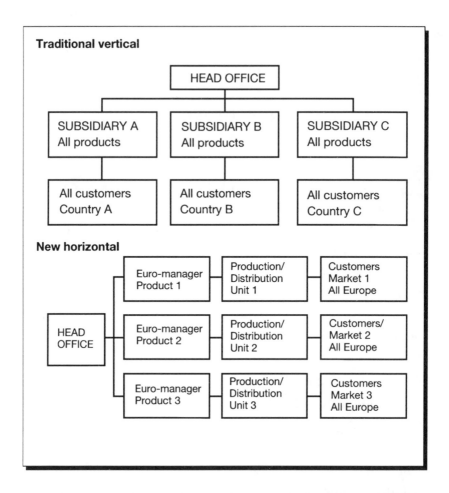

management styles can best be harnessed if Product A is con-trolled from Athens, Product B from Birmingham and Product C from Copenhagen. All can then see that if they are to have their plans implemented everywhere without hassle, they must not be obstructive of other people's.

Certainly there will be for some time to come a shortage of managerial staff with a broad enough combination of interna-tional experience, management skills and languages. The Business Schools will continue to do their best, but there can be no substitute for field experience. Wise companies may prefer to groom existing key staff fast by a combination of internal training, cross-posting and short 'hot-house' external courses.

CONCLUSIONS

In 1967, Jean-Jacques Servan-Schreiber wrote *Le Défi Américain* to warn that European business was in danger of takeover by the giant American multi-nationals. Twenty years later, a much greater danger appeared to come from the Japanese industrial conglomerates. Yet with the '1992' initiative, the European Community has set about creating the opportunity for European-based corporations to build a home market as big as that enjoyed by the USA or Japan, and which will act as a base from which an attack on world markets can be mounted with at least an equal chance of success.

All businesses – whether they realise it or not – already have a strategy for the Single Europe. Doing nothing (or 'wait and see') is one alternative, but not to be recommended. Even a business with no ambitions to sell outside its traditional home territory must assume that new EU-based competitors will be interested in its customers. Indeed those customers may themselves decide actively to exploit the new opportunities to seek cheaper, more innovative or more responsive suppliers. As KPMG Peat Marwick wrote in their Euro-brochure: 'Those who fail to develop a strategy for 1992 will ultimately be forced to react to changes imposed by suppliers, customers, financiers, investors, competitors, all of whom will be responding to the opportunities of the Single Market.'

This necessity for good strategic planning has not been

changed by the Single European Act, only its perspective. A Single Europe which provides a 'home market' of eventually over 500 million people, enlarges many times over the scale of opportunities now offered by single countries of 10–50 million; but simultaneously multiplies the problems. Hence the continued need for sound marketing: companies offering a good product to a strongly based customer franchise can look forward to long-term success. The less well founded will probably disappear during an inevitable competitive crisis in the medium term.

The winners will therefore be market driven, with a detailed knowledge of the needs of their present and future buyers and how best to satisfy them at a profit. The key to success will be to understand as fully as possible the nature of the business decision taking process and to identify the 'Euro-buyers', namely all members of the DMU in each potential customer.

A surviving and successful company will be one able to anticipate the changes because it has *researched the situation, modified its offer and marketing approach* and above all, *broadened its attitudes* through being led by *Euro-minded and Euro-trained* managers.

19

HOW TO HANDLE INTERNATIONAL ADVERTISING

'The essence of multi-national marketing is not simply formulating strategies for particular national environments. Rather it is operating simultaneously in more than one national environment, co-ordinating these operations, and using the experience gathered in one country for decisions in another country . . . a demanding task'

(Harvard Business Review)

CAN WE BALANCE LOCAL NEEDS AGAINST THE BENEFITS OF CENTRAL CONTROL?

As pointed out in Chapter 18, the world is becoming more regionalised, and few companies can survive by selling only in their country of origin. As more goods cross borders, so does the need grow to market and advertise in other countries whose languages, local customs, legal requirements and ways of doing business will differ considerably. Inevitably, a company marketing multi-nationally will need specialist advisers (such as advertising agencies, market research consultancies, lawyers) and more and more commonly will choose one with a network of local offices in the relevant countries. The handling of international business by such agencies requires diplomacy, common sense and experience – backed up by watertight administration.

Experience indicates that for the agency–client relationship to work effectively, the agency network and the responsibilities of each of its individual offices must be tailored to match each particular client's marketing needs, structure and politics.

THE RISE OF THE 'NOT INVENTED HERE' SYNDROME

Structure and politics have to be considered because the growth of international alignment and co-ordination of advertising and other marketing activity have inevitably increased the degree of central control demanded by the advertiser's Head Office over such key issues as corporate image, strategy and budgets – at the expense of local management.

Local management deeply resent this loss of control and inevitable curbs on their ability to control their own operations and to hire and fire their own agencies:

> *'We understand our market – they do not.'*

> *'How can people sitting in New York or London produce a strategy relevant to Germany, Hong Kong or Australia, let alone all three of them?'*

> *'How can I be responsible for meeting my profit target, without full control over the essential marketing techniques such as advertising?'*

Some such arguments may just express the NIH (Not Invented Here) syndrome, but others may have a point.

THE PROBLEMS OF THE CENTRE

Common problems in developing internationally co-ordinated

marketing and advertising, created by an inexperienced, insensitive or over-rigid centre, are:

1 Lack of willing agreement and enthusiastic execution from local managers used to local autonomy
2 Ambiguous channels of communication between Head Office and subsidiaries, and between each office and its agency
3 A tendency to give priority at all times to the needs of 'big' countries over smaller ones
4 Insisting on extending ideas from countries where they work to others where they do not, on grounds of administrative convenience or apparent cost savings
5 Letting apparent similarities between countries override differences, especially where the latter are more important to the market than the former
6 Ignoring the fact that the techniques appropriate to sophisticated markets will not work, and may not even be available, in less developed ones
7 Danger of not making full use of, overriding or even ignoring local knowledge and expertise, thereby demanding the impossible of local management and turning their potential help into guerilla warfare.

OVERCOMING THE PROBLEMS

The starting point in solving these problems is to recognise their existence. Too much talk of 'the global village', flying visits to capital cities and negotiations exclusively with senior foreign executives who have graduated from international business schools, can give an impression of closer convergence in ways of life and doing business than would be gained from longer stays and deeper contacts with the workforces of local associates and customers.

There are many benefits that can be gained by central co-ordination, but also disadvantages, and the trick is to find a way of combining the expertise of the centre with local knowledge of market conditions.

Fig. 19.1 Centralised and decentralised control

Decentralised	Centralised
Pros	*Pros*
On-the-spot knowledge	Control of funds
Greater motivation through autonomy	Control of corporate image
	Control of style
More relevant advertising	Control of content
Directed at specific local needs	Synergy of communication
	Buying power
Cons	*Cons*
Short-termism	Out of touch with local market
Danger of fragmented, contradictory or weak corporate image	Inflexible, slow to react
	Bland, lowest common denominator
Reinvention of the wheel	Demotivation of local management
Total dependence on variable local skills	
Little control over budget	

The answer is likely to lie in balancing the degree of authority that is exercised from the centre, with the amount of input and consultation permitted to those working on the ground. The more strategic the issues, the more a company's operations in different countries will have in common; the closer to their tactical execution, the more it will be desirable or even necessary to permit local variation. As Chapter 18 put it – 'Think Europe (or world-wide): act local.'

MAKING IT WORK

The starting point for action depends on whether the company concerned is organised on what Chapter 18 called a vertical or horizontal structure.

Where local subsidiaries have autonomy for budgets and sales, within perhaps a centralised framework only of patents and trademarks and corporate demands solely to hit guideline targets for return on capital or profit on turnover (called a 'vertical' structure in Chapter 18), centralised co-ordination of advertising can be no more than an advisory function. Co-ordinators will try to encourage synergy through joint consultation and will communicate to local failures case histories of successes in other countries, but will have no powers to insist on their adoption.

In such cases, a centralised network of advertising agencies can exacerbate the political embarrassment, whereby the client co-ordinators expect the agency to put pressure to conform on its local clients through its branches. This puts the agency into the position of international policemen, with a consequent deterioration in agency–client relations both centrally and locally.

It is better under such circumstances, if a multi-national agency is appointed, that its branches are granted the same degree of local autonomy as their clients. These agencies can then devote themselves to serving local needs, but retain access to central resources and expertise when the need arises. Regular consultation and sharing of experience will in practice encourage voluntary trial or adaptation of other countries' ideas, with only a minimum of NIH.

Where a company is organised 'horizontally', with responsibility at a single point for targets and budgets for a product throughout a region, it becomes almost impossible to control marketing activity *unless* the agencies are co-ordinated in the same way as their clients. The agency has to have the resources and flexibility in operating to be able to give strategic advice in whatever country (and city) the advertiser's top manager is, with a full executive facility in every country where marketing takes place.

GUIDELINES FOR SUCCESSFUL CO-ORDINATION AND CONTROL

1 Agree the principal objectives of co-ordination:

- consistency and strength of corporate and brand image
- improved management and allocation of resources
- cross-fertilisation and sharing of ideas, to speed development and avoid repetition of mistakes
- avoidance of duplication
- cost savings through economies of scale
- common standards

2 Agree whether centralised or decentralised co-ordination is required.

3 Tailor the agency's structure and responsibilities to meet client requirements.

4 The agency to appoint a senior executive as 'international management supervisor' responsible for:

Fig. 19.2 Co-ordination

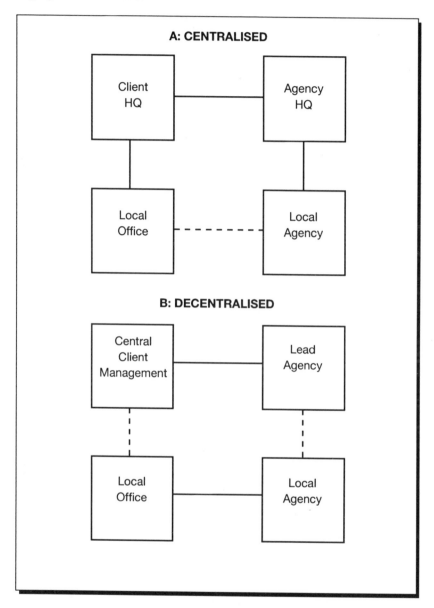

- providing a single point of contact for management and Head Office
- co-ordination
- maintaining standards
- keeping information flowing freely between offices
- maintaining administrative disciplines
- ensuring that each office benefits from the experiences of others working for the same client.

5 Agree clear-cut lines of authority and approval.

6 Develop an 'operating procedures manual' for the guidance of all client and agency offices. To include (for example):

- corporate objectives, strategies and identity
- client structure with names and responsibilities
- agency structure with names and responsibilities
- working procedures, including:

    (i)   briefing
    (ii) lines of approval
    (iii) invoicing
    (iv) currencies
    (v) terms of business
    (vi) standard requirements, such as contact reports, schedules, proofs.

Much of this is of course no more than normal agency–client relationships on a somewhat larger scale. As the number of people increases on both sides of the fence who have first-hand multi-national experience and good language skills, operating in several countries simultaneously will become second nature.

But in the short run, those with the skills and experience will be in short supply and those without will be best advised to put themselves in a position to learn from them as soon as possible.

20

CONCLUSIONS

THE 'FIVE QUESTIONS'

The Introduction posed five fundamental questions, which are asked by business management with increasing frequency of their advertising and marketing advisers:

1 Which is most important to success: good advertising or a good product?
2 What does success really mean?
3 Can success be guaranteed in advance?
4 Should advertising be treated as a current business expense or a long-term investment?
5 On what basis should a marketing budget be set, and how should it best be divided between alternative activities?

Such questions do not (of course) have universal answers, valid for all businesses and all markets for all time. This book has addressed itself to various alternative approaches, and will have justified its existence if readers have been able to clarify their own answers, in the light of the situation in which they find their business. It has discussed a number of issues which have to be clarified before reaching valid answers.

BUSINESS-TO-BUSINESS v. CONSUMER MARKETS

This book is primarily aimed at readers who operate in business markets (which many consumer market operators still refer to as 'industrial'), although its approach is not unknown nor inapplicable to consumer markets (which many business market operators still refer to as 'retail').

The most usual difference is a matter of scale: usually the quantities ordered by a business customer are very much larger than by a domestic household, and the number of customers to be serviced is very much smaller. The number of people involved in most business buying decisions is also much larger, although the mechanisms concerned with identifying a need and choosing a supplier are often surprisingly parallel between the DMU in a business and in a domestic household.

This is because the decisions in either case are taken by *people*, who take them on the basis of their knowledge about what is available and on what terms, to satisfy their needs. However, there is a great difference in the channels by which people seek information when they are choosing for themselves or choosing for their business. In consequence, there is a wider choice of marketing techniques likely to be cost-effective for business suppliers, and the structure of such a campaign will almost always be more complex than one aimed at households.

So, while marketing has many generic characteristics across the business/consumer divide, it cannot be assumed that any approach to marketing communications developed in a consumer context is automatically applicable to business-to-business. It is not wise for management selling to businesses to seek advice from practitioners whose expertise has been gained solely in consumer markets.

THE BASIS OF SUCCESS IN BUSINESS

The basis of success for any commercial company, stripped of all jargon, is to find customer firms with needs which the supplier can satisfy, to identify the people in each such firm who will influence a decision to buy, and to communicate to them the information they need in order to take it in favour of the supplier's brand. This book has recommended the techniques and approach of marketing in general and of marketing communications in particular as a basis for doing this, and has distilled much practical experience in how to make them work profitably.

IS MARKETING DEAD?

Yet, at the time of writing this chapter (mid-1994), the UK marketing trade press was full of articles claiming that marketing as a discipline had reached its 'sell-by date'. To be fair, much of this appears to relate to consumer marketing. Typical headlines were 'demise of the brand manager', 'marketing hits mid-life crisis' or even 'death of brands': backed by stories of big-name companies closing marketing departments and laying off brand managers in favour of 'customer liaison teams'. In further support, they quoted anecdotal cases of spectacular failures of expensive launches of new packaged goods or of blockbuster sales promotions, of brand leaders pulling out of highly visible marketing activities, of multiple retailers stealing the customer franchises (and much of the brand values) of long-established lines.

Inside knowledge often reveals that such failures were brought about without benefit of marketing professionals or against their advice, that the apparent spending cuts have been diverted into expansion of other marketing activities which are harder for the media to monitor or cost out and that powerful retailers had been allowed to get away with activity which would have led straight to court if done by a direct competitor.

The business-to-business sector adopted modern customer-orientated marketing somewhat later than the market leaders in fast-moving consumer goods. Here at least (to adapt Mark Twain) reports of the death of marketing have been much exaggerated. Certainly marketing as 'a fancy name for selling and advertising' has been moribund for decades. But according to its professionals, marketing is an approach to doing business, not a set of techniques. Marketing is about customers; or more precisely, about using the resources of a company to satisfy its customers' needs at a profit.

Without a body of loyal customers any company will wither away. Whether those responsible for identifying good customers, understanding their needs and designing cost-effective ways of fulfilling them are called a marketing department, a customer liaison team or Father Christmas is irrelevant providing they are properly recognised as the guardians of the company's survival, profitability and growth.

WHY SHOULD MARKETING BE UNDER THREAT?

On this definition, the function of marketing is as necessary as it has ever been, and nowadays has access to techniques to make it even more successful than in the past. The problem has been that since the development of customer-orientated marketing in the 1960s, the top management of businesses (both consumer and industrial) have been progressively distracted away from their true role of creating wealth through satisfying customers' needs.

Their attention has been diverted to dealing with successive economic crises, the establishment in many markets of a pro-active distribution chain, intervention by governments and numerous single-cause anti-business lobbies, the rise of investigative journalism and the intensification of international competition. All these have led to a squeeze of margins due to (inter alia) rising costs, expensive money, high taxes, over-supply, stagnation in growth of demand and unpredictable fluctuations in buyers' choice of suppliers.

It is paradoxical that in such a disastrous combination of circumstances, companies who have never before felt the need to use marketing often turn for the first time to marketing advisers to help them out, while companies with long-established marketing departments usually expect them to make the biggest contribution to every cost-cutting exercise. It is conventional (if short-sighted) for management to ask marketing to bear a disproportionate share of cut-backs in budget and staff when recession strikes: but it adds insult to injury if at a later date they accuse their by then chronically under-funded and short-staffed marketing function of failure!

Indeed, the distraction of senior management away from the needs of their customers has been dignified by such terms as 'trade marketing', 'environmental marketing' and 'media issue management', which help to make respectable the diversion of funds once devoted to new product development, the reinforcement of brand images and rewards for customer loyalty, into attempts to placate ungrateful distributors, indifferent politicians, fickle institutional investors and media more interested in high profile news than boring reality.

Obviously, such problems have to be addressed, but surely not at the expense of the customers who are the sole source of most companies' income. In any case, distributors deal most eagerly with the suppliers of high-quality products in strong demand; while legislators, financiers and the media listen most respectfully to the managers of successful, expanding, profitable and market-leading goods and services.

MAKING MARKETING PAY FOR ITSELF

It has been the thesis of this book that marketing (at whatever level and under whatever name it takes place) is an essential function of a successful, profitable business. But, as a direct consequence, all marketing activities can and must justify themselves as effective and cost-effective, at least to the same extent that any other business activity has to.

The corollary to this thesis is that whenever marketing does satisfy management's pre-set criteria of profitable contribution to sales, management should then authorise for it the necessary funding and the autonomy to get on and do its job; just as they do for production, distribution, finance, media relations and other line or staff functions.

The various chapters have given some principles or at least 'points of entry' to help marketing management to develop and demonstrate cost-effectiveness for a variety of aspects and techniques of marketing; and some criteria to help those responsible for funding and policy to assess the contribution of such work in achieving business goals. It offers a philosophy which suggests answers to the 'five questions' which apply at least in business-to-business marketing.

THE 'FIVE ANSWERS'

1 Good advertising or a good product?

Answer: you cannot live on either without the other! Advertising does not work in isolation, and cannot be used on its own to create success. Heavy advertising which generates widespread trial of a poor quality or inadequate product is one of the fastest ways of driving it from the market. Getting the product 'right' is therefore the first priority on funds. But in most markets there are many products on sale which are 'of merchantable quality' and competitively priced. To persuade buyers to switch, they need to be made aware that a product exists which will satisfy their needs better in some way than their current choice. Advertising is one of the most cost-efficient ways of telling them.

2 What does success really mean?

Buying advertising is a business decision just like any other. Money should be spent on advertising or extra staff or new machinery or a marble statue in the foyer if and only if the total benefits in the long term are greater than the total costs. If by objective criteria any activity does not 'work', it is a waste of money.

Advertising works if, and only if, it achieves its stated objectives. It is *successful* if it achieves them cost-effectively, that is, if it produces a profit above all the associated costs. Businesses which have regular monitoring systems for their marketing activity and take consistent action on the results will have increasingly successful campaigns.

3 Can we guarantee success?

There are no guarantees of success in business – or we would all be millionaires! All commercial profit comes from taking risks, and the higher the profit required the higher the risk that must be taken. Business risks cannot be eliminated, but it is the job of marketing management to identify and assess the risks in the marketplace and to balance them against its potential rewards as far as possible. In the case of advertising, the best ways of doing this are by analysing the market and competitive situation realistically, by pre-testing all new activities and by learning progressively from experience. The litmus test is to compare the most likely final outcome with and without advertising (or with alternative ways of spending the money), and going for the one that promises the best 'bottom line'.

4 Is advertising a tactical expense or a strategic investment?

While advertising can be shown to have both short-term and long-term effects, a great deal of recent quantification goes to show that advertising is at its most successful when used consistently to build brand and corporate images, leading to customer loyalty in the long term.

Yet the accounting practices of most companies demand that advertising must be classified as an expense and written off within a financial year. This leaves advertising vulnerable to tactical cost-cutting, and consequently 'eating the seed corn' of customer goodwill in times when competition is heaviest.

5 How should a marketing budget be set and how divided by activity?

Setting a sensible budget for marketing as a whole depends on getting realistic answers to four questions:

(i)   What do we want our marketing to achieve?
(ii)   What would that be worth to us if we succeeded?
(iii) What can we do with that sum to achieve the objectives?
(iv)   How likely is that plan to work?

If the answers collectively make sense in the light of known market conditions, then the indicated budget is a good business risk. If not, both the objective and the budget need to be reassessed.

Allocating the agreed budget between activities should be done against different criteria. Calculations should be made objectively of the likely end-result of spending the budget in appropriate alternative ways of achieving the desired objectives: such as price cutting, advertising, customer promotions, additional sales staff, better after-sales services (and indeed not spending the money at all).

However, the short-list of candidate activities should be short. Each marketing technique is more appropriate in some contexts than others, and each acts on the customers in a different way. If several techniques seem equally appropriate, this would suggest that the objectives are too vague and need to be made more specific.

If (for example) a company were to switch all its marketing budget from image advertising to direct mail in the following year, this would imply a U-turn in objectives, or some kind of crisis within the market, because these two techniques are not interchangeable and do very different jobs. It would seem much more likely that the company would need to use both advertising and direct mail strategically, but might well switch the emphasis between them tactically if (for example) a campaign consisting mainly of couponed advertising had built up a good list of potential customers; which might lead to a need to establish a dialogue with them by mail with image advertising cut back to a holding weight.

THE KEYS TO SUCCESS

The keys to success in advertising (and other marketing activities) are:

(i)   set realistic *goals for sales and profits*, based on an objective analysis of the marketplace

(ii) set specific and *quantified objectives* for the whole marketing function, arising from the business goals of the company and co-ordinating it with other activities, and *budgets* agreed to be adequate to achieve them

(iii) before approval, relate advertising and other proposed marketing activity to these objectives and budgets, and agree on '*action standards*' for their success

(iv) set up *monitoring systems* to track the required effects of each approved activity, and continuously feed back their results to all those involved

(v)   *regularly review* the situation by meetings between management, and the internal staff and outside agencies or suppliers who carry out the work. The reviews are to evaluate results on an objective basis with the intention of reinforcing synergy and minimising weakness

(vi) continuously *fine-tune* the tactics of each activity as new information demands, but *maintain the strategy* unchanged for as long a period as market circumstances permit.

Long and broadly-based experience has not only helped to develop these guidelines, it has also shown in practice that those who follow them consistently become progressively more effective and cost-effective in their marketing campaigns. This shows up in higher sales, at better prices, from increasingly satisfied and loyal customers, and leads to a better reputation, improved profitability and a higher valuation of the whole business on its balance sheet.

Advertising (and the rest of the marketing mix) is a cost unless it sells, but if it does so it will protect the company's profits in bad times and spearhead its growth in good.

INDEX

Further titles of interest

FINANCIAL TIMES

PITMAN PUBLISHING

ISBN	TITLE	AUTHOR
0 273 60561 5	Achieving Successful Product Change	Innes
0 273 03970 9	Advertising on Trial	Ring
0 273 60232 2	Analysing Your Competitor's Financial Strengths	Howell
0 273 60466 X	Be Your Own Management Consultant	Pinder
0 273 60168 7	Benchmarking for Competitive Advantage	Bendell
0 273 60529 1	Business Forecasting using Financial Models	Hogg
0 273 60456 2	Business Re-engineering in Financial Services	Drew
0 273 60069 9	Company Penalties	Howarth
0 273 60558 5	Complete Quality Manual	McGoldrick
0 273 03859 1	Control Your Overheads	Booth
0 273 60022 2	Creating Product Value	De Meyer
0 273 60300 0	Creating World Class Suppliers	Hines
0 273 60383 3	Delayering Organisations	Keuning
0 273 60171 7	Does Your Company Need Multimedia?	Chatterton
0 273 60003 6	Financial Engineering	Galitz
0 273 60065 6	Financial Management for Service Companies	Ward
0 273 60205 5	Financial Times Guide to Using the Financial Pages	Vaitilingam
0 273 60006 0	Financial Times on Management	Lorenz
0 273 03955 5	Green Business Opportunities	Koechlin
0 273 60385 X	Implementing the Learning Organisation	Thurbin
0 273 03848 6	Implementing Total Quality Management	Munro-Faure
0 273 60025 7	Innovative Management	Phillips
0 273 60327 2	Investor's Guide to Emerging Markets	Mobius
0 273 60622 0	Investor's Guide to Measuring Share Performance	Macfie
0 273 60528 3	Investor's Guide to Selecting Shares that Perform	Koch
0 273 60704 9	Investor's Guide to Traded Options	Ford
0 273 03751 X	Investor's Guide to Warrants	McHattie
0 273 03957 1	Key Management Ratios	Walsh
0 273 60384 1	Key Management Tools	Lambert
0 273 60259 4	Making Change Happen	Wilson
0 273 60424 4	Making Re-engineering Happen	Obeng
0 273 60533 X	Managing Talent	Sadler
0 273 60153 9	Perfectly Legal Competitor Intelligence	Bernhardt
0 273 60167 9	Profit from Strategic Marketing	Wolfe
0 273 60170 9	Proposals, Pitches and Beauty Parades	de Forte
0 273 60616 6	Quality Tool Kit	Mirams
0 273 60336 1	Realising Investment Value	Bygrave
0 273 60713 8	Rethinking the Company	Clarke
0 273 60328 0	Spider Principle	Linton
0 273 03873 7	Strategic Customer Alliances	Burnett
0 273 03949 0	Strategy Quest	Hill
0 273 60624 7	Top Intrapreneurs	Lombriser
0 273 03447 2	Total Customer Satisfaction	Horovitz
0 273 60201 2	Wake Up and Shake Up Your Company	Koch
0 273 60387 6	What Do High Performance Managers Really Do?	Hodgson

For further details or a full list of titles contact:

The Professional Marketing Department, Pitman Publishing, 128 Long Acre, London WC2E 9AN, UK
Tel +44 (0)71 379 7383 or fax +44 (0)71 240 5771